Truckin' with Sam

State University of New York Press
Albany, New York

Truckin' with Sam

*A Father and Son, The Mick and The Dyl,
Rockin' and Rollin', On the Road*

BY LEE GUTKIND
WITH SAM GUTKIND

Portions of the chapters on Africa were originally published in the Travel Section of the Washington Post, September 20, 2009.

Portions of this book are adapted from my earlier book *Forever Fat: Essays by the Godfather* (Lincoln: University of Nebraska Press, 2003). Grateful acknowledgment is made.

Published by
State University of New York Press, Albany

For information, contact State University of New York Press, Albany, NY
www.sunypress.edu

Production by Kelli W. LeRoux
Marketing by Fran Keneston

Library of Congress Cataloging in Publication Data
Gutkind, Lee.
   Truckin' with Sam : a father and son, the Mick and the Dyl, rockin'
and rollin', on the road / Lee Gutkind with Sam Gutkind.
      p. cm.
   ISBN 978-1-4384-3259-5 (hardcover : alk. paper) 1. Alaska
Highway—Description and travel. 2. Alaska—Description and travel.
3. British Columbia—Description and travel. 4. Yukon—Description and
travel. 5. Gutkind, Lee—Travel—Alaska Highway. 6. Gutkind,
Sam—Travel—Alaska Highway. 7. Fathers and sons—United
States—Biography. 8. Fathers and sons—Alaska Highway. 9. Pickup
trucks—Alaska Highway. I. Gutkind, Sam. II. Title. III. Title:
Trucking with Sam.
   F1060.92.G88 2010
   917.9804'52092--dc22

                                                            2009051679

10 9 8 7 6 5 4 3 2 1

◙ ◙ ◙

We wish to dedicate this book
to Gary Paulsen,
the author and adventurer,
who inspired our truckin' odyssey.

◙ ◙ ◙

Contents

Preface

"What's All This Blood, Dad?
I Don't Understand!"

IT MAY SEEM ODD—counterintuitive, even—to preface a book about father-son bonding with a story about discovering my mother's menstrual blood. My editor, in fact, initially advised against it. But sometimes insights come in the most unlooked-for places. So, here goes:

I am seven years old and living in a tiny walk-up apartment with my parents in Pittsburgh, Pennsylvania, and I see in the toilet one morning what seems, to me, to be a bucket of blood. I panic.

My father left for work an hour ago, but my mother has been in the bathroom most recently, so I run out into the kitchen, where I think she is making breakfast, screaming, "Ma! Ma!" The radio is on, with one of her favorite programs, "Don McNeil's Breakfast Club," but she's not there. So that increases my panic level to full-blast. She said she would be in the kitchen. And at this time of day she is always in the kitchen, and so I expect her to be in the kitchen, and she is not in the kitchen. So now she is missing. And I am thinking, "Is my mother lying somewhere a bloody mess? Is she dead?"

She's not in her bedroom, nor in my bedroom, nor in our little living room. No blood spots anywhere I look, either. I check the closets. I peek under the beds. I look in the drawers and the cupboards, just to be thorough. No Ma. No blood.

So I run downstairs and out onto the porch. And thank God, there's Ma, talking to Mrs. Doris Lindenbaum, her best friend, at the time. My mother's best friends come and go in cycles. They are in and out—and in—as is Doris Lindenbaum now, the best friend of the moment.

And of all of the women I remember as friends of my Ma, Doris Lindenbaum is my favorite because she has a kaleidoscope of blue lines on her legs, which are called, says my mother, "varicose." When my mother has poker games at our house, usually the first Thursday of the month, I sneak into the kitchen and, when no one is looking, crawl down under the table, cluttered with chips and cards and coffee and Coke, and I study the lines of varicose that Doris owns.

My mother's other best friends have varicose, too, but Doris beats out everybody. Doris is tops. There's a map of the world on Doris' legs—snaking every which way—from ankle to knee, to that place way up under the tunnel of her dress where those dark, alluring mysteries lurk. At some point a few years later, I will learn from an older boy to refer to this secret under-the-dress spot as "Joy City." But even when I am only seven, I know deep in my heart that there is something warm and wonderful going on up there, under that dress, that will someday yield unforgettable pleasure.

So I see Doris Lindenbaum on the porch that day. It is early. But I don't have the patience to wait to say to Mrs. Lindenbaum, "Excuse me," or "How are you doing, Mrs. Lindenbaum? How is good old Marc?" Marc is her son who is in my grade at school. An odd sickly kid; gets beaten up all the time. Or, "What are you doing here so early in the morning, Mrs. Lindenbaum? Will you join us for breakfast?"

And neither do I have the patience or the good sense to say to my Ma, "Can I talk with you privately, Ma?" or "Ma, can you spare a moment? I'm a little upset and I need to ask you about a few matters pertaining to a bucket of blood I found this morning in the toilet." You know, something preliminary.

All I know is that my mother may be bleeding, losing all that blood, and if she's bleeding, she may be dying, and if she's dying, I am going to be a boy without a mom, which is going to make me upset and change my life.

I have a dad. But I don't want to be with my dad if my Ma isn't there to protect me, because my dad, he's alright sometimes, but he tends to get violent when things don't go well, and even when things do go well, I am, in addition to being the only child, his designated family punching bag, whenever he gets those urges. And my dad, he gets a lot of urges. Upsets real easy.

Unless, of course—and this is something that occurs to me as I momentarily hesitate on the porch where my Ma and Mrs. Linden-baum are talking very quietly—women pee blood. I have never seen a woman pee before, I suddenly realize. I have never seen a woman's penis before, either. I haven't the slightest idea if women own penises, and if they do, if those penises are like my penis or Marc Lindenbaum's penis or gigantic like my father's penis, which, compared to my little weenie, is thick as a tree trunk. Or what if they poop blood, those women? An additional possibility.

I know that women are different than men. Men pee yellow. I pee yellow. My father pees yellow. Everybody I have ever known, all the boys and men, pee yellow—yellow or whitish-yellow. The bus driver who takes me to synagogue Sunday school tells his favorite joke about the book he is reading, "Yellow Streams" by the famous author I. P. Daily. I assume that I. P. Daily is a man. And I get the joke, which is kind of funny the first few times you hear it. But then there's this blood in the toilet. What's with that? Yet my mother looks perfectly healthy right now. Do women pee red, I wonder, as I stand out there on the porch with Mrs. Lindenbaum, and I am yelling, "Ma! Ma?"

Then this next thing runs through my head, out of the blue: Women have those big soft balls on their chests that we boys in school call bazoongies. When I have seen them, my mother's bazoongies are usually covered in elastic, and they've got points that make them look like torpedoes. They are very interesting, those torpo-zoongies. "Why don't men have bazoongies?" I ask my father.

My father sells orthopedic shoes for a living, so he is considerably more comfortable discussing bunions and metatarsals than torpo-zoongies. I am the only kid in school who knows more about longitudinal arches and ingrown toenails than Christopher Columbus discovering the world is round and the Pilgrims landing at Plymouth Rock. I am intimate with the workings of the fluoroscope, which provides an x-ray of your foot to make certain your new shoes fit. In my closet, I have Buster Brown scuff toes for school, Poll Parrot wing tips for dress-up, U.S. Keds for softball, rubbers for rain, and four-buckle arctic boots for snow. "It is not respectful to use that word," my father says.

"Bazoongies?" I say, after a while. "Torpo-zoongies?"

My father is very uncomfortable with anything, he says, is not "on the straight and narrow." His definition of the "straight and narrow" is rigid—to the point of abolishing all curves—maybe especially on women. And he is not known for his sense of humor. Fathers must maintain a position of maturity and dignity, he insists. "You mean 'breasts,'" he says.

"Why do women have breasts and men not?"

"Men do have breasts—small breasts," my father says. "And nipples."

"Nipples?"

"Nipples are at the very tip of the breasts, like a little button."

"But what's these big breasts? Those pointed pillows?"

"Breasts," my father says—and here he pauses for dramatic emphasis. There seem to be stars in his eyes. "Breasts are beautiful things."

This is exactly what my father says when he tells me about the word "fuck." This is three or four years later, and I ask him what the word, "Fuck" means.

"Fuck," he says, pausing and looking away from me, "Fuck is a beautiful thing."

"Fuck is beautiful? Then why I am put in detention because I and my friends have 'fuck'-yelling contests to see who yells the word 'fuck' the loudest in public? Why do people get mad when you call them a 'fucker'?"

"That's a different story," my father says.

"'Fuck' is different than 'fucker'?"

"Someday you will understand," he says.

This stays with me my whole life. Something I never forget, like the anticipation of visiting Joy City. *Fuck* is a beautiful thing. *Fuck* is different than *fucker*. *The act itself is good and the perpetrator of the act is bad.* Fatherly wisdom at its finest—sort of. And in retrospect, as I look back on my life, I consider this the ultimate gem of enlightenment from my dad—a rare magic moment of connection and legacy. Nothing my father ever told me resonates more clearly in my memory.

My shrink, Dr. Mason, asked me once, after my first marriage collapsed, and I came to him, desperate, lonely, and helplessly impotent, who and what do I think about after having a satisfying sexual experience? "I don't have satisfying sexual experiences any longer. Why do you think I am paying you these big bucks?"

"Well, when you did have satisfying sexual experiences, what went through your mind? Or who?"

"My father," I say, thinking back to my enlightenment when I learned the truth about the yin and yang of the "F" world.

"Your father?" Dr. Mason writes that gem of evidence and ammunition down in his spiral notebook and shakes his head vigorously, encouraging me to continue. His eyes light up. This will be worth another year of weekly sessions, at least. I can hear the cash register in his brain dinging. All in all, that guy will suck me in for nine years.

"Then what do you think when you think about your mother?" he then asks.

"Blood."

"Blood?" he says, taking another note. I imagine he is drawing stars and exclamation points and dollar signs in his spiral notebook around this note. This is why ordinarily nice people, good citizens, become shrinks. All the dirt they learn from their clients. They eat it up, write it down, read it aloud in the middle of the night, it turns them on so much. Much better than being priests because, ethically, the shrink can still fuck, which, as I mentioned, is a beautiful thing. "You want to kill your mother?" Dr. Mason asks.

"Blood and my English teacher," I tell him.

"You want to kill your English teacher, too?" Another note. I think I see his hands are shaking.

Now I tell him about the bucket of blood in the toilet. I tell him how I ran downstairs and burst out onto the porch and blurted out my panicked question: " Ma there's blood in the toilet. Are you dying?"

I remember how my mother looked at me in shock that morning, how her eyeballs got big and round. "What are you talking about?"

"Please don't die," I said. "I don't want to become an orphan."

It just so happens that my mother and Mrs. Lindenbaum had been talking about death at that very moment. Perfect timing. Mrs. Lindenbaum's son Marc was dying. He had leukemia. There was no cure. I didn't know Marc was dying at the time I burst out onto the porch; I found out later. But this is why Mrs. Lindenbaum, Doris, was at our house so early, to talk with her best friend. She couldn't sleep at night. She felt alienated. She craved comfort and support.

I wish I could have given Doris Dr. Mason's phone number, for she needed him more than I did. A son's leukemia is considerably more traumatic than a horny guy who can't get to Joy City, even when the doors are wide open.

"And your English teacher? Why your English teacher?" Dr. Mason said.

"Because my mother told me that what I had seen was a period. Her period. Although at the time she said, 'a period.'"

Thinking back, she had evidently not flushed the toilet so thoroughly—or maybe not at all—I figured. Mrs. Lindenbaum was suddenly at the door, knocking, a surprise visit, so my mother rushed to answer. Soon thereafter I stumbled into the bathroom, and, well, now you know what happened next: panic and confusion.

"You went to your English teacher and asked about a period?" Dr. Mason smiled and wrote some more notes.

"Yes," I said, "I needed to know the truth about this blood."

"How did your English teacher explain period?"

"She said it was a punctuation mark."

"When did you learn the truth?"

"You mean that's not the truth?" I said.

"Why didn't you ask your father?" Dr. Mason asked after a while.

"I couldn't rely on my father. He would have told me, 'A period is a beautiful thing.' I needed hard facts."

Dr. Mason took down another note, and nodded, as he tends to do as an encouragement for me to speak. But I didn't say another word. We stared at each other until the session ended. It turned into a long, quiet afternoon.

◎ ◎ ◎

THAT EVENT—my accidental discovery of my mother's period and the absolute panic it precipitated—happened long ago. But I can still remember how foolish I felt years later when I finally understood what had occurred that morning in the bathroom—where the mysterious blood had come from—and why.

I only wish I had been given a reasonable explanation back then. My mother told me that I was mistaken; that there was no blood. "You are imagining things!" I knew that wasn't true—and I wasn't imagining Marc Lindenbaum's death, either—but I could have just as well imagined it, for his death was barely noted in my house or anywhere else. Marc left the world and our school without collecting his final grades or emptying his locker. All that was left of Marc, all I could get from my parents later when they were leaving the house one afternoon in dress-up clothes, were four words: *Sitting shiva for Marc.* Figuring out what *shiva* was took a couple of years.

When I was growing up, parents were less open and communicative with children, tending to shield them from the realities of life. As to "sexual" matters—intercourse et al (and the "F" word)—parents mostly thought that there'd be plenty of time for kids to learn about "Joy City" when they were mature enough to handle it which, in the 1950s and early 1960s, was supposedly in their mid- or late teen years—or, alas, in some cases, in their early twenties. This was wrong, I think. Kids of any era need to know when they need to know. They won't follow a timetable established by parents or society—curiosity invariably wins out and often with harmful effects.

Today, cable TV and the Worldwide Web have made shielding children from life's lessons and realities impossible, and I don't think I benefitted from my ignorance back then. Growing up, I devoted a great deal of time and effort to trying to understand what the adult world was all about. Why do we fear communists? ("Because they're bad.")

Why do we keep our distance from black (colored) people? ("Because they will steal from you.") Why are the Jews persecuted—and why do I have to be a Jew anyway? ("Because we are the Chosen People.") And, of course, if "fuck" is so beautiful, then why is saying the word so bad? And, by the way, what's with all that blood in the toilet?

Parents don't have to tell their kids everything—but they ought to be trusted and reliable sounding boards, always accessible and always willing to tell their children the truth. Hiding information or providing misinformation even with the best of intentions is usually unhelpful or detrimental. This trusting, bonding relationship is in many ways more important and more fragile between fathers and sons than mothers and daughters. Men are more rigid, generally, less forgiving and understanding.

In past times, bonding between men was more natural; fathers often taught sons skills with their hands on the family farm or through repairs around the house. They talked as they worked. Breakfast and dinner—holidays, weekends—were shared. Now it takes a lot of planning to connect the lives of different generations. Passion for computers and games like *Sim City* and *Civilization* frequently replace a shared love for baseball or other all-American pastimes. Family outings are rare. And these days, fathers must think a lot more carefully about what it means to be a man. Today, we embrace individuality. Flexing muscles no longer trump the flexing mind. What kind of man—what kind of person—do I want (do I want my son) to be?

I think it was the disappointment I felt with my father and my general disillusionment with family life that led to my initial decision to not become a parent. Both my first and second wives were on the same page; they had their own family issues. But I changed my mind—later in life—at 47. That's one major theme of this book—becoming an "old new dad"—and the advantages and difficulties this role presents.

"Old new dad" is a term I first learned from Mark J. Penn. In his book, *Microtrends: Small Forces Behind Tomorrow's Big Changes*, Penn devotes a chapter to "Old New Dads." Whether children come from birth or through adoption, "old new dads" are part of a growing worldwide movement, he says. In the United States a quarter century ago, men over fifty were responsible for one in every twenty-three births. In 2002, the figure climbed to one of each eighteen births. Birth rates from fathers between ages of forty and forty-four increased nearly one third, and for fathers forty-five to fifty, the group where I fit, birth rates increased twenty per cent. Recent studies in the U.S. and Europe show that more than one in ten of all children are born to fathers forty and older, one fifth of whom are over fifty. Being part of this movement—an old new dad, as I am—requires considerable emotional and physical

adjustment. Old new dads need to learn to minimize our obvious inse-
curities: We are older than most of our kids' friends' parents and might
not so easily fit in; our cultural references are generations behind our
children's; and we have more ghosts from our past to deal with. Old
new dads must learn to maximize our special advantages, namely, our
more secure financial and professional positions and the wisdom we've
gained through experience, fighting battles and dealing with demons
that younger men have yet to confront.

I won't say that my past came back to haunt or motivate me when
Sam was born because long before Sam I was thinking about the positive impact my father could have made in my life if he had been more
active and communicative. His distance created a void and a resentment
I carry with me even now. I know I am not alone. So many men were
and are denied the intellectual and emotional substance needed to
shape their personality and to deal with the challenges of growing com-
fortably into male maturity because their fathers were too preoccupied
with their work or too rigid in their beliefs about hanging tough, not
revealing emotions and feelings to their sons for fear of showing weakness and vulnerability.

As you will see, "truckin'" became a metaphor for the father-and-
son bonding experience, a way of communicating and coming together
to teach, to share, to grow—and have fun. In addition, in an odd way,
truckin' also became somewhat of a religion to Sam and me, as we
shared the irreplaceable awesomeness of the Grand Canyon, the elation
of the crystal blue ice field atop Exit Glacier, the haunting ghosts of
Auschwitz and Theresienstadt, the anger of Hebron on the West Bank,
the eerie exotic weirdness of being trapped—foreigners in Tibet—
during the rumble of revolution, and then, finally, a month before he
was to enter college, after truckin' together faithfully off and on for six
years, the ultimate test we both confronted—a culmination of all I had
tried to communicate to him in ideas and attitude and all I had learned
about being a father and setting a fitting example through trial and
error as an old new dad—in East Africa, in Tanzania of all places.

But whether you are traveling, as Sam and I so often did, or sitting
in the backyard, togetherness—or truckin', as it is defined here—is the
message of this book. It is an imperative of fatherhood. Nothing can or
should interfere with establishing a connective tissue between father
and son, expanding it, growing it, following it, holding on to it until the
proper time to let go. Literally or spiritually—and preferably both—all
fathers, everywhere, of every age, must go truckin' with their sons.

Prologue

Africa—July 2009

THE SCENES ARE VIVID, unforgettable, perhaps even more so because, not having been close enough to see the accident itself, I have had to painfully and carefully reconstruct it in my mind based on what Sam and others have told me. The images dance in my head repeatedly each day, like a video on continuous rewind and playback, frame by awful frame:

There is Sam, speeding along the highway, losing control of his bike, flying through the air and smashing headfirst into a wall of gravel and rock. His helmet is cracked in four places and the plastic that covers the helmet is shredded. Even imagining the sound of the impact is enough to make me sick to my stomach. I bite hard, down into my lips, tasting blood. I want to hurt myself so that the hurt won't transfer to him.

And there is Sam, up on his feet but staggering, his sock and boot soaked with blood, his back throbbing and bleeding, while the truckers who had stopped to help were yammering at him in Swahili and asking him for money to take him to the next town. For a short while, he couldn't remember where he was. He was in shock. So was I.

And next, there is Sam, slumped in a wheel chair in the casualty ward at Kilimanjaro Christian Medical Centre, dazed, pale, nervous, and still very bloody, and then there is me, running up and down the hospital corridors, trying to get someone to pay attention to him—and to me—someone who spoke English.

On the outside I am calm, showing Sam a confident and reassuring smile, but on the inside I am frantic, repeatedly questioning my judgment and my sanity for having committed us—or more precisely, my son—to such a senseless, irresponsible, unnecessary experience.

And finally the doctors—two men, tall and slender, black faces accentuated by their white lab coats: They say that Sam probably doesn't have a concussion; his temporary loss of memory is from the shock of the collision, and the wounds on his back, now that they had been treated, will heal in time. But the gash in Sam's ankle cannot be stitched. Plastic surgery will perhaps be required.

I am relieved, of course, but my heart sinks, selfishly, because I want to complete this entire experience with my son—biking through the interior of Africa and then climbing the magnificent Kilimanjaro, Africa's highest peak, Hemingway's monument to obsession—to stretch ourselves once again before Sam immerses himself in the second act of his life in college. The doctors are politely (but not definitively) recommending that we consider packing it in—go home.

But Sam is not prepared to acquiesce to injury. He makes it perfectly clear to the doctors and to me that he intends to climb Kilimanjaro, no matter what.

I have such mixed feelings at that moment. I want to tell Sam that I think that perhaps he is being foolish, that he could really endanger himself, further injuring his ankle and his many other wounds, and that his weakened and vulnerable condition could cause annoyance and disruption to the other half-dozen members of our little group.

But I want to also tell him that I am proud of him, all the same. While I do not want my son to be cavalier about himself and others, I also do not want my son to be a quitter. I listen as he talks with the doctors and I don't say a word. I figure he is truckin' by himself at this point, and I really can't—and don't want to—do a damn thing about it.

PART I

The Open Road

Portal

North Dakota—June 2004

WE WERE ABOUT seventy miles north of Minot, North Dakota. It was mid-morning, chilly and gray, and we had been driving for a little more than an hour since breakfast. As we barreled up the flat, four-lane highway waffled with weather and neglect, we seemed to be the only people in the only vehicle on the road.

"This is eerie," Sam said.

"Erie is to the east. This is North Dakota," I said.

"You're a jerk, Dad," Sam said.

"Thanks Sam," I replied. "I appreciate the significance of your comment."

This is the little routine Sam and I frequently perform—part of our Sam and Dad *schtick,* like an oft-repeated Vaudeville vignette. I say something stupid, he tells me I'm a jerk, and I feign appreciation and recognition in response. Being a jerk is good in Sam and Dad lingo. We have a similar routine for the word *schmuck.*

Sam might say something inappropriate or silly, and I will reply, "You're a schmuck, Sam."

And Sam will say, "Thank you, Dad. I appreciate your gracious acknowledgement."

Bystanders don't understand—and we don't tell them—that in Sam and Dad lingo, "schmuck" means "great man."

AT PORTAL, NORTH DAKOTA (pop. 131), the sign read, "You are leaving the United States," and then the wide blacktop narrowed down to a lonely two-lane roadway. There were some buildings up ahead, and we could see a couple of vehicles parked in the shadows behind them. We slowed at a guardhouse the size of a telephone booth expecting someone to step out and say or do something official, but the hut was empty. We stopped and waited perhaps a minute or two, alone and in silence.

As planned beforehand, Sam activated the video camera to record the exact moment our truckin' odyssey across Canada and over the famed AlCan, the Alaska-Canadian Highway, 4,000 miles from here to Homer Spit, the westernmost portion of the continent, began.

"I guess we can go," I said. "I'm anxious to AlCan," I added.

I shifted into drive and slowly accelerated, heading up the roadway, which is when the moment we had been waiting for—the official beginning of our AlCan odyssey—suddenly became the moment of our potential undoing.

"WAIT!" a voice exploded from nowhere. "WHERE THE HELL DO YOU THINK YOU'RE GOING?"

I jammed on my brakes, stopped our Toyota Tundra in the middle of the road, and sat, gripping the steering wheel, frozen. Then a very large man in a blue tunic, spit-shined boots that went up to his britches, and an automatic revolver in a leather holster strapped to his waist, emerged from the building behind the hut. As he approached the driver's side door, he bellowed to Sam: "TURN THAT DAMN CAMERA OFF." Then he paused as he glared into my window. "WHERE DO YOU THINK YOU ARE GOING?"

"Canada?" Stupidly, I replied as if it was a question. I heard my voice crack—and I turned away from Sam so that he could not see how flustered I was. "And Alaska," I added.

"IDENTIFICATION!" he barked. I wondered if he was actually angry or if this was an act to scare the living shit out of me. I had heard from a Canadian friend that the border guards—the officers of the Canadian Customs and Revenue Agency—at smaller crossings were a nasty bunch because they were posted so far away from civilization. Either way, his threatening bluster was working. It was all I could do to control my shaking fingers as I fished my wallet out of the inside pocket of my Levi's jacket and flipped it open to my driver's license.

"WHY DIDN'T YOU WAIT? THE SIGN SAYS 'WAIT.' YOU *DIDN'T* WAIT."

"I didn't see the sign," I confessed. "I'm sorry. But I did wait for a minute," I added.

"IDENTIFICATION?" he repeated.

"It's right here," I held up my wallet like a white flag.

"TAKE IT OUT AND HAND IT TO ME."

I wanted to say, "I can hear you; your shouting is giving me a headache," but his size, his neatly pressed uniform with a sparkling gold and blue badge and a garish shoulder-flash with the world "Customs" represented in French and English—not to mention his shouting—continued to intimidate me. I didn't dare to look at Sam in the passenger seat, who, I was certain, was expecting me to take some definitive action to put this guy in his place.

"WHO IS THAT?" he pointed at Sam.

"My son, " I said. "Sam," I added, thinking that attaching a name to the face of a cute thirteen-year-old would soften his tone. Sam was very slender and pale, with light brown hair flowing in jagged bangs on his forehead—maybe a shade over 5'2"—and glittering braces on both rows of teeth. In the mornings he obsessed over those braces—floss, rubber bands, brushing, etc.—often causing friction between us, especially on school days, over how much time he takes in the bathroom and how early he has to get up in order to deal with the many complications of adolescent ablutions. But there's something inside of Sam, always has been, an anchor, a stabilizing force, a moral and intellectual center that elevates and separates him from the rest of us—and even from me. Sam's sedate aura seemed to have a mellowing effect.

"May I see your identification, Sam?" the guard asked in a more cordial fashion.

But I realized even before Sam turned to look at me for guidance that though the guard had softened his tone, the situation was getting more untenable. "He doesn't have identification," I blurted. "He is only thirteen; he can't drive; he doesn't have a license."

Now the guard's eyes narrowed into bright intense beams. "Does Sam have a passport?" he said through his teeth.

"Yes."

"Let me see it." He held out his hand and I paused to take a breath. I noticed that the word "Customs" was represented in English first on the guard's badge and French (Douanes) second, but on the shoulder-flash the translation was reversed. I assumed that this was an attempt to achieve total egalitarianism, but the guard was becoming even more impatient as I pondered.

"Passport?" he repeated.

"It's at home," I confessed.

"Does he have a birth certificate?"

I shook my head, overcome by a wave of nausea generated by my own ineptitude. I swallowed and choked: "Home."

The guard was silent now, but his eyes asked the obvious: *How could you be so stupid?*

As the guard continued to question, I felt the most horrible sinking feeling coming over me. I had worked so hard and planned so carefully for this trip with Sam from Pittsburgh up the AlCan and beyond—an entire summer for a father and son to bond. And now this dream of experiencing something pioneering and adventurous and over-the-top-incredible, together, was suddenly in jeopardy. If only Sam would have said at that moment, "You're a schmuck, Dad," I would have felt better. But Sam was silent.

"How do I *know* that he's really your son?" the guard continued his interrogation.

"I guess you have to take my word for it." I was now nearly whispering I was so dismayed.

"Do you have permission to take this child out of the country?"

"Permission? But I'm his father."

"Are you also his mother?"

"Yes, I have permission from his mother," I said, anticipating his next question and ignoring the question he asked.

"Where is this so-called permission?"

"Where is it? It's nowhere. I mean," I hesitated, not knowing what to say. "His mother knows what we're doing." I stopped, swallowed. "Sam lives with me," I blurted, realizing that this information had no relevance, but feeling obliged to say something of substance.

"You're not married?"

"Divorced."

"Do you have proof?"

I was tempted to answer, "Of divorce?" But I thought better of it. "You mean *proof* that his mother has given me permission to take him out of the country?" I asked.

"Proof in writing," he added.

"No," I said. "I don't."

"You were not aware that you needed identification to go from one country to another? That children are kidnapped, taken away from their parents or parent and smuggled into other countries? For reasons I won't even talk about," he persisted, 'in front of Sam."

"Of course I knew that," I said. "But I thought I didn't need documentation to enter into Canada."

"Why did you think that? Who told you?"

"I called the U.S. passport office," I said.

I actually couldn't remember who provided this information, or, to be truthful, if *anyone* had provided any information. Perhaps I had imagined it. My mind was suddenly blank.

The Evolution of Truckin'

IT ALL BEGAN in a Starbucks near Sam's school—with a book I was reading to Sam. This is what we do after school most every day. I get my coffee, he snacks on pizza from the Italian Village across the street on Forbes Avenue in Pittsburgh, and I read aloud. We read in the morning, as well, at a diner, Ritter's, a Pittsburgh landmark, where Sam has been eating the same breakfast almost every day since beginning grade school. Sam gets pancakes, a scrambled egg (well done), bacon, and milk. As soon as we walk into Ritter's and settle into stools at the counter, a waitress invariably turns to Charlie, the short-order cook, and yells, "Put Sam on the grill!"

I can't tell you how many books we've read together—quite a few—and it's a real eclectic mix. We've read Lauren Slater's *Opening Skinner's Box*, for instance. Sam was interested in Skinner and the box in which he allegedly locked his daughter to test "operant conditioning." Sam is a geek—he loves science and technology, so we've read Rodney Brooks, Stephen Hawking, Richard Preston, and Charles Darwin. But all sorts of literature intrigue him. We've read the Greek philosophers, large chunks of the Old Testament, and short stories and essays from John Steinbeck, Isaac Asimov, Madeline L'Engle, and Ernest Hemingway, among other writers.

Once, a woman approached our table in blue scrubs and stood and listened as I read "Indian Camp," a story in which Nick Adams, a character Hemingway based on himself, observes his father deliver a baby to an Indian by caesarian section only to learn that the newborn's father has committed suicide during the procedure. When I finished, she said,

"My dad read me 'Indian Camp' when was I was young and I decided right away I would become a doctor. It inspired me. Your son will be inspired by something you read to him, too, one day."

In *The Car*, a young adult novel by Gary Paulsen, the book that initially inspired our truckin' experiences, teenager Terry Anders is abandoned by his parents with a few dollars, a couple of loaves of bread, and a "kit" car his father was in the process of building, called a Blakely Bearcat, which Terry nicknamed "the Cat." Terry finishes building the Cat and begins driving to Portland, Oregon, to search for a long-lost uncle. On the road, he meets two nomadic Vietnam vets, Waylon and Wayne, who quiz him about literature, history, and contemporary American culture: Terry is clueless. Wayne and Waylon conclude that he needs to be educated—to see America—so, on the spot, they propose to take him "Truckin'."

Before *The Car*, Sam and I already had the habit of driving around the city aimlessly, listening to the radio, a routine we still follow even now with Sam at eighteen, but back then we finally found a word or a metaphor for it: *Truckin'*. And with the word, the possibilities became more vivid—at least to me. We weren't just seeing sights when we were driving around, I told Sam; rather, we were *truckin'*—as in the classic song of the same name by the Grateful Dead:

Truckin,' got my chips cashed in.
Keep truckin', like the doodah man.
Together, more or less in line,
just keep truckin' on.

I assumed that Waylon and Wayne were Deadheads—and I made the connection for Sam by talking in depth about the entire rock-and-roll era, beginning with The Grateful Dead but moving expansively back and forth in time.

So from that point onward, Sam and I went truckin', taking longer and longer sojourns, listening to those whispering echoing sounds of my past—Mick Jagger, Jerry Garcia, Bob Dylan, Jim Morrison. Sharing their music with Sam, it seemed as if I was just this moment discovering them myself. Dire Straits. Mark Knopfler. The music was turning me on all over again! Why—when—had I stopped listening? I wondered. How could I have forgotten the compulsive passion of these tunes that had once so inspired me?

Whereas I was prone to sing along with the music, sometimes at the top of my lungs, Sam consumed it all in silence. He was happy to talk about the artists—personal details about the vocalists and the bands—but avoided conversation about the sound and the lyrics. It put him in a trance. As to the "Truckin'" song, the concept interested him much more than the song itself. Truckin', I told Sam, could be interpreted as a metaphor for spontaneity—a lack of restriction. "Truckin' means that you can do what you want to do sometimes; you don't always need to do what is expected."

"Like taking a shower?" Here he saw a way out of a responsibility he found annoying and senseless.

"Well, it is important to shower every day; it's an unavoidable thing that people do. Like breathing. Eating. You keep yourself clean. But, if, one day out of the blue, you decide not to shower, well? So?"

"So you're truckin'," said Sam.

"Breaking the rules. Changing the pattern. Going with the flow."

"Like watching *Volcano*," Sam said.

This was Sam's favorite movie of the moment. We were into disaster movies at the time. We watched all of the *Airport* movies made in the 1970s (five of them) along with *Dante's Peak, The Towering Inferno,* and *Twister*—repeatedly—and then we talked about them incessantly, mostly about how stupid and unlikely they were. In *Volcano* or *Dante's Peak*, the stars, Tommy Lee Jones and Pierce Brosnan, respectively, could outrun or come dangerously close to rivers of lava, thousands of degrees hot, showing hardly any effect. "They should be boiling! They should be dead and disintegrated, and they are not even sweating!" we would yell at the TV monitor. "Why are they stopping to kiss [the leading ladies were Anne Heche and Linda Hamilton] when they could be saving thousands of lives?"

What always amazed us about these disaster movies is how quickly and neatly they ended. In *Volcano*, hundreds of thousands of people are probably dead, the city of Los Angeles is in ruins and it will take a quarter century to rebuild it, but now it is raining, which magically cools down the lava, and Tommy Lee Jones and his teenage daughter, who had been working in a hospital caring heroically for casualties during the disaster, are holding hands, while Anne Heche and Tommy are smiling and looking at each other in that very alluring way—a promise of passion in Joy City in the very near future.

All of which brings me back to this afternoon at Starbucks when I began to hatch a plan to make the idea of truckin' a reality—an on-the-road adventure for Sam and me to share on a number of levels—a multiple bonding experience—music, reading books, male camaraderie, with a little geography and history, educational components, rolled into the package.

For a while, I began to think about recapturing my motorcycling days by buying a new BMW and truckin' on two wheels. I had sold my old BMW, the one that had taken me all around the country while working on a book about the motorcycle subculture, a few months after Sam was born because, quite surprisingly and suddenly, after two decades of riding, I didn't feel safe anymore. Motorcycling became scary—a gamble not worth the danger.

Every time I got on my motorcycle, I began to think that something terrible was going to happen, that I would smash up and die before I saw Sam, again. Or worse, I'd be mangled and twisted in an accident, and then I'd be wheelchair-bound, a quadriplegic. who could only talk to Sam by blinking my eyes or biting on a computer cable and transmitting artificial voice sounds—a Stephen Hawking–like figure, without Stephen Hawking's fortitude and intelligence. So motorcycles weren't in the cards for Sam and me, but I concluded that if I was really going to entice Sam into truckin', which I suddenly seemed to be doing, it would have to be in the right way and in the right vehicle, which was, necessarily and undeniably a truck.

Everything that happened in Starbucks from that point on just seemed to happen spontaneously, although I have to admit that there was a certain amount of scheming behind it. We were sitting there, Sam and me, talking, and while we were talking, I snatched a discarded newspaper from an adjoining table and leafed through the pages in the Want Ads section. I hadn't discussed this idea—I hadn't even worked it out in my own mind. But I was responding to this nugget of an idea of cementing my relationship with Sam.

My eyes were on the Used Trucks for Sale section of the paper. I spotted an ad for a 1998 Ford Ranger four-cylinder pick-up, very clean, only used for gardening, and I showed it to Sam as I slipped my cell phone out of my jacket pocket and punched in the phone number, all at once, but casual-like.

Jeff—the owner of the Ranger—was home, working in his garden. "He's a middle-school teacher," I tell Sam. I am talking with Jeff and Sam, back and forth, Jeff at home, Sam beside me. "Jeff once taught at St. Edmunds," I tell Sam. This was Sam's school.

"Jeff says that he only uses the truck to haul mulch." Jeff lives fifteen minutes from where we are sitting.

"We can come over and test-drive the Ranger right now, this very minute, if we want to."

I look at Sam and raise my eyebrows. Sam looks back and smiles. "Jeff," I say into the phone, "we're on our way."

Chasing Madness

ON THE FIRST MORNING of our AlCan adventure, several days before the border-crossing incident in Portal, we drove north toward the Pennsylvania–New York border, then headed west into Ohio. We traced the Lake Erie coastline until I found my oasis in the desert—Starbucks. I had had plenty of coffee through the morning, but nothing invigorates me like Starbucks coffee, an injection of adrenaline that I can feel seeping through my arteries the moment I take the first sip.

The thing about Starbucks is that it is always the same, wherever you go. No surprises. The coffee tastes the same, the uniforms of the baristas, the tables and chairs, the napkins and sugars, even the flooring, kind of a flagstone like tile, is pretty much the same, state-to-state, Starbucks to Starbucks. I love the paper cups—I always get a double cup, one cup on top of the other, so that I don't have to get a sleeve—the sleeves get stuck in my cup holder. I can't stand coffee shops that serve coffee in a Styrofoam cup, and I can't stand coffee shops where you have to dispense your own coffee from a thermos. I don't believe in thermoses. I want my coffee thick, black, and bold, right out of the urn. "Raw and wild," I tell Sam.

Growing up in Pennsylvania, I had always heard about the wonderful tour of the Hershey Chocolate factory in which you could watch the entire chocolate-making process unfold while eating as many Hershey's kisses—"silver tops" we called them—as parents allowed. And one of my favorite writers, John McPhee, wrote an article for The New Yorker about a man who had worked for Hershey's as a taster.

Right before chocolate was about to be poured into molds, bars, or kisses, this fellow would sample each batch and, when determining that the taste and consistency were of acceptable quality, would announce, "That's Hershey's." Later, in Arizona, we will learn about how the Indians in the Sonoran desert made their wine from fruit that grew on top of the saguaro cactus, simmering in leak-proof baskets for nearly a week until the rich brew was proclaimed ready to drink by the medicine man known as "the keeper of the smoke." That's how I feel when I sip a Starbucks. It is coffee the way I want it—the way coffee is supposed to be, no matter what anybody else says. When it comes to coffee, I am the keeper of the smoke.

THE COUNTRY FLATTENS OUT as you move from hilly Pennsylvania into the Midwest. The landscape stretches out in front of you taut, like sheets on a bed.

Once, I tell Sam, when I was in my early twenties, I fell in love with a girl, Roni from Toledo, Ohio, where we are passing at that moment—The Glass City—they made more automobile windshields than anywhere else in the world in Toledo back then!—and I would drive back and forth, Pittsburgh to Toledo, like a maniac, like Dean Moriarty and Sal Paradise, the narrator of *On the Road*, scampering lunatics, coast to coast, just to have a date with Roni, and then I would drive the four hours back to Pittsburgh that same night to get to work the following morning.

I wanted Roni so much at that time in my life; thoughts of Roni day and night, visions of Roni as my wife, the mother of my children. But now, I don't remember hardly anything about Roni, except that she was Jewish, she was short, and she attended Ohio State University. How could I love someone, be crazed over someone as much as I was crazed over Roni and be totally out of touch with her today? Even if I saw Roni on the street (maybe I did see Roni in the street today), I would not know her. "It was the madness of the chase," I say to Sam, who gives me a blank look, having totally spaced out in the blaring music—The Beatles, The Eagles—completely unaware of what I am talking about, and answers, "Yeah." He puts his forefinger on the dial of the CD player. "Mind if I turn up the volume?"

WE HEAD NORTH towards Chicago. "My father, Jack," I tell Sam, "hitchhiked to the Chicago World's Fair from New York, in 1936. He was twenty-two years old. Later, he went to Clarksburg, West Virginia, to work in a shoe store. This was during the Depression. Jobs weren't easy to find. You went where the work was. In Pittsburgh for a weekend visit, Jack met Mollie. They were engaged in three months."

Here was another instance of chasing madness: my parents' whirlwind courtship. It is difficult to conceive of the passion that propelled my father to bump and swerve six hours and 150 miles in his 1928 Ford on Saturday nights after work on half-paved West Virginia roads to see my mother on Sundays and then to turn around and retrace his path to be back Monday morning. In the eighteen years I lived with them and during all of my visits for family events thereafter, I can't remember Mollie and Jack touching. Not a single handhold; not one kiss.

In the second floor walk-up apartment where we lived, you could stand on a ladder in the bedroom closet behind my father's hanging suits and find a window-sized door that opened into a tiny attic. Here were boxes of heavy black phonograph records, thick with dust: recordings of operas with great performers like Mario Lanza and Ezio Pinza. There were old yellowed books about communism, Zionism, political dissent, filled with my father's faded pencil scrawl—evidence of a level of engagement that was completely unrecognizable in the father I knew.

WE PICK UP INTERSTATE 80, which connects to Interstate 90, which connects to Interstate 94, which connects to Interstate 29, from Ohio through Illinois and Wisconsin. We stop now and then, to eat—and to listen, capturing snatches of conversation, momentary interactions between other travelers.

A middle-aged husband with a Caterpillar baseball cap to his wife: "Did you have a dream last night about Samurais?"

"I don't remember. Why?"

"You shot up out of bed in the middle of the night and hollered, 'Bonsai!'"

A grandfather to a teenage boy: "Grandma's got that bag (colostomy) on her side and sometimes that smells real bad—you know what I am saying? Don't mention nothing—it will hurt her feelings."

A woman to her husband in a hotel lobby: "Did you see the key to the room—a plastic card!"

Boyfriend: "The worst thing I ever did in my life was drink a bottle of diet Mountain Dew with an expiration date of 1997."

Girlfriend: "I am tired of hearing that damn story."

We have been talking about computers, cell phones, condoms, and sex—in no particular order.

"Wrap that rascal," a phrase I picked up in the military, gives Sam a kick. I explain the feeling of sex with and without condoms. I talk about STDs, premature ejaculation, impotence, and masturbation. "STD," I tell Sam, "is different than STP."

WE DON'T KNOW the name of the young man sitting two tables behind us, but he is articulate and earnest, discussing the important issues in the world today, such as the challenges posed by AIDS in Africa, the ongoing tension in the Middle East which, as he puts it, could "lead to catastrophic actions and reactions" and turn the world into a "self-igniting incinerator." He is not ultraliberal, by any means, for he supports President Bush's "liberation" of Iraq and is troubled by the rise of criticism by Democrats, reported incessantly on TV and in the newspapers.

Not that his insights are unique; it's all been said before, from one point of view or another, on the Sunday morning talk shows, in newspapers, bars, diners, and street corners. But despite being around the same age, this young man is different from the university juniors and senior I teach because of his social passion, knowledge of current events, and sense of history, depths, and dimensions that many of my students lack. I recently asked a class of fifteen students to name the vice president of the United States. Two could not answer. I followed up by asking for the name of the man who ran against President George W. Bush in 2000. Four were clueless. Exasperated, I told one of the two students who had missed both questions that Al Gore had invented Gore-Tex. "I wasn't aware of that," she said.

But more than this young man's social passion and sense of history is the fact that he is having this conversation with his parents. Sam and I can talk about any subject with passion—and disagree congenially. But my friends with teenage children tell me that change is afoot, just around the corner. They've battled their teenagers into adulthood over every issue imaginable and through enduring periods of brooding silence and revolt. "You wait," I am warned. "In high school their behavior is intolerable and in college it is much worse."

I hear what they are saying, which is one reason why this young man, perhaps nineteen years old, clean-cut, bright-eyed, makes me feel so good. There he is, sitting calmly and discussing and sharing the issues that matter to him—*with his parents!*—and seemingly enjoying himself. I am hoping that Sam is taking note of this conversation and that it is making an impact on him.

Coincidently, Sam and I are leaving at the same time as the young man and his parents. They are in two cars. Before they say goodbye, the boy assures his mom that he has a good dinner planned for later—"a double meatball hoagie."

"I am happy to hear that," she says. "You have to eat well and stay healthy."

The mom and dad depart, but the young man, in the parking lot, walks slowly to his car. I watch him carefully from the driver's seat of the truck—still glowing inside with the thought that such a nice, enlightened young man exists as kind of an imaginary model in my own mind for Sam, someday, the teenager, not far into the future.

The young man is carrying his cup of Coca Cola from the restaurant, and he sips it thoughtfully as he reaches through the window of his old Chevrolet and takes a small item out his glove compartment. At first, I can't make out what it is. He walks around to the driver's side and leans against the door, looking reflectively and moodily into the distance. Then he finds a book of matches in his shirt pocket and lights up his joint, the item procured from the glove box. His eyes are closed and his head rests back against the roof of his car, as he exhales into the sun.

As you travel north, the country becomes more frigid and barren. In Pittsburgh the sun was shining the day we left. But in Minnesota snow was still visible on the shoulders of the road and wind beat a rattling, vibrating drumbeat on the roof of the cab. The wind got so bad in North Dakota that it ripped the end of the tonneau cover from the bed of the pick-up. We eventually had to stop and buy bungie cords to clamp the tonneau down. The further north we cruised, the flatter the land, the fewer the trees, the grayer the horizon. The people: weathered, wrinkled, plain, dour, and glum.

"Wonder what it would be like to live here," Sam said as we entered Fargo, North Dakota. The city is located on the Red River, a narrow, muddy blanket of water separating Minnesota and North Dakota. A sign says that there are 99,000 residents in Fargo and that the Fargo City Hall is located at 200 3rd St. N., downtown.

"I've been here before," I told Sam, "on my motorcycle. I went into a bar and ordered a beer, put a ten dollar bill on the bar, and went to the men's room. When I got back, the beer was there—Budweiser—and my change, with the bartender standing right in front of where I was sitting. 'You're from Pittsburgh,' he said.

"'How did you know that?'

"'Only people from Pittsburgh are dumb enough to walk away from their money on the bar and expect it to be there when they get back.'"

Sam is nodding, maybe listening and maybe not. The Doors are rocking and rolling as I am speaking. Jim Morrison is talking about how he doesn't believe in astrology and horoscopes. He admits that he is a Sagittarius, "the most philosophical," but given that, "It is a bunch of bullshit," he says. He believes in rock and roll—which is a lot more interesting than my Fargo anecdote, I admit.

We follow the interstate past Fargo to Jamestown, North Dakota, then eventually connect to US 52, which takes us to Portal. North Portal, a sister city, is just over the border in Saskatchewan. Some time later, I Googled Portal and learned that the town is known for its international golf course, the only course in the world in two countries, with the first eight holes in Canada and the final hole in both countries. You tee off in Canada and your ball crosses the 49th parallel and because of the changing time zones lands in Portal, North Dakota—an hour later.

Trapped at the Border

THE BORDER GUARD pointed at a parking space in front of a large corrugated metal structure. "Back your truck between those two yellow lines. Leave your possessions and come inside."

I followed his directions, my hands shaking as I maneuvered the truck as he had directed me. I turned off the ignition, paused to reach over and rest my hand on Sam's knee to reassure him.

"What's going to happen, Dad?"

"I don't actually know, Sam," I admitted. I didn't say any more because I felt a feeling of defeat and helpless paranoia creeping up on me.

As we walked from the truck into the larger building behind the guardhouse hut where the border guard had directed us and sat down in the tiny waiting area near his office, I glimpsed the imaginary newspaper headlines in my hometown. "Canadian Border Guard Captures Pedophile from Pittsburgh. Reputable Writer and Professor Foiled in the Act of Kidnapping a Child."

I pictured my colleagues in the English Department where I teach huddled together at the mailboxes, where they often gather to gossip, concluding that my true evil nature had finally been revealed. I could hear them whispering to one another, imagining them nodding vigorously, proclaiming, "There was always something about Lee that wasn't quite right."

We waited around in a small reception area decorated in government gray with cheap plastic chairs and tables with pamphlets about immigration and duty free items and other stuff that did not interest us. The guard had disappeared into a back office.

As we waited, I began to understand what I had done wrong. The border crossing point at Portal was not particularly busy, so the officers sat inside in shirt sleeves, doing paperwork, and when a vehicle turned up, they finished what they were doing and went out to perform their border guard duties. They assumed that people would see the sign to wait—and that they *would* wait. I had evidently not waited long enough. Or I didn't see the sign.

Or perhaps I did, on second thought. Perhaps the sign was big as a house and I had looked right at it, but it didn't register. Middle age gives "missing" or "not seeing" or "not acknowledging what you see" a new dimension of meaning. Sometimes you see what you are supposed to see, but your mind is so full of other matters in the checklist of your life (Do I have enough fuel? Did I make the phone calls I promised? Have I answered my e-mails? Did Sam get enough to eat and drink?) that what you see doesn't register on the screen of your present reality.

Of course, Sam didn't see the sign, either. Or, if he did, he didn't alert me to it. But he's a kid, and so he is not the responsible party. I am the father, and performing these adult-like, seemingly simple chores, like taking us into Canada from the United States without being hassled by border patrol guards in blue tunics and spit shined boots, is my responsibility. That's what dads do.

"Do you know how much longer this will take?" I asked the woman border guard behind the front counter. She dropped her pencil, looked up from her paperwork, and paused, scanning me up and down. Clearly, she didn't like what she was seeing: a white-haired, Levi's-clad hippie, with a generous nose, a crinkled face, and a blue turquoise earring snug in my left lobe, trying to steal an innocent child from his mother. Her eyes fixed on that turquoise nugget as if it were a telling symbol of my debauchery.

"Officer (she said the name of the guard who had detained us) is making the phone call now," she said.

IN ABOUT FIFTEEN MINUTES, the guard returned carrying a fax that Patricia, my ex-wife, Sam's mom, had sent, providing permission for me to take my son into another country.

"So does this mean we can go?" I asked.

"No," he replied, "It doesn't."

We went out to the parking lot to our truck—a dark red Toyota Tundra V-8. The Ranger had performed well, but we had traded it in. The Tundra was more powerful and spacious—suitable for the AlCan.

The nerf bars—shiny chrome steps, like running boards—looked cool, too. No one at the truck accessory store had any idea what "nerf" meant. The best we could figure, based on the meaning of "nerfing" in computer gaming, meant that the bars made it easier and less complicated to get into the truck—which made sense.

The guard directed me to unload the truck and line up all of our possessions in the parking area so that a German Sheppard dog could sniff our packs and suitcases for drugs. A second guard in a blue uniform and black boots, just like the first guard, swept over everything with a metal detector. Since I was going to give a workshop and a reading at a writers' conference, I had a couple of boxes of books and journals—a fact that prompted the guard to ask, jokingly, "Porno?"

"Not in the same truck as Sam," I said.

"Just because you have been permitted to enter Canada," the first guard finally said after the dog completed its sniff test, "it may not be so easy to get back into the United States."

"What do you mean?"

"The U.S. border guards can be more suspicious than we are," he replied: "This is a warning," he said. "Just wait.

SAM WAS KEEPING a truckin' journal to record his own observations of our experiences. Here is what he said, in part, about our first few days in 2004, heading toward the AlCan:

Around Chicago, my dad was annoyed because he thought that I had not been paying enough attention to navigation. But I got out my GPS and map, where I found that we were on track, exactly where we should have been. My dad is also annoyed because our GPS-to-computer cable is not compatible with any of the adapters on my notebook computer. My dad said that I should have thought about this ahead of time. He is constantly nagging me to think ahead.

The border patrol at the border from North Dakota into Canada was not too happy with us. There was apparently insufficient proof of my identity and relationship to my dad. We should have brought passports. And we needed a written authorization from my mom saying it was OK to journey on to Canada. The officer telephoned her. She wrote a note and faxed all this to the border guard. The officer was mean in the beginning, but a nice person in the end and allowed us into the country. But my dad should have been thinking ahead, like he is always telling me.

Listening to the Road

WHEN WE TRUCK, we talk. I've got a lot of stuff about life, love, lunacy, etc., on my agenda to tell Sam, so in the truck I go on and on until I can sense that he's had enough of his father's wit and wisdom and he shuts down. Only so much a kid wants to hear from his dad at any given time—then they tune out.

We also listen to books on tape. The first two years truckin' we immersed ourselves primarily in Harry Potter, books five and six, *The Order of the Phoenix* and *The Half Blood Prince*. We devoted three hours most every day, more or less, listening to—almost literally living inside of—Harry's Hogwarts world, with Albus Dumbledore, the wise headmaster, Severus Snape, a reformed Death Eater, and the mysterious and evil He Who Must Not Be Named, while simultaneously watching the country go by, the houses, the billboards, the trucks and trailers, and the parade of humanity—old, young, whiskered, wasted. A couple of years later, in another truckin' trip, Sam and I would discover that there's actually a real life He Who Must Not Be Named in another part of the world—the Dalai Lama—in Han-occupied Tibet.

But rock and roll remains the highlight of the ride and the way to begin and end the day. Every day, we start with the Grateful Dead and "Truckin'." No deviation, no way, because we wouldn't be having these adventures without the partial inspiration from Jerry Garcia and company. "Are you ready?" Sam will say first thing, when we get into the truck. Sam injects the CD into the changer, selects the third track on the "Best of The Grateful Dead" album, presses the button, and the music begins. Sometimes I sing the opening—

Truckin'—got my chips cashed in.
Keep truckin' like the doodah man.
Together, more or less in line . . .

—or I try. Singing is not one of my strong points. Sam proposed a rule that I could only sing after we listened to the song in silence at least twice. So I got the hint.

Then, after "Truckin'," Sam will select a Rolling Stones CD—we've got maybe ten of them, including *Flashpoint, Sticky Fingers,* and *Forty Licks,* three favorites, and we listen as we enjoy the scenery and the brightening of the morning. That's usually our first hour—maybe even two hours, if I am able to get in some narrative insight about the country or stuff in the news to discuss that I have picked up from TV. After the first Stones album from beginning to end, and I really mean "beginning to end," for Sam refuses to miss a track on any of the Stones we play—and furthermore if a track is interrupted, like for a bathroom break or a phone call, or if I dare to speak while The Mick is crooning, then Sam, the purist, will insist we start the track at the beginning, and listen all over again, and only after every track is consumed will we go on to some other album.

We listen almost exclusively to rock and roll (Janis Joplin and Jim Morrison and The Doors are regulars), with a little bit of contemporary folk-rock mixed in (Fiona Apple, Jill Sobule, and The Flaming Lips), some pure folk (Simon and Garfunkel and "The Dyl"), Joan Baez, Emmylou Harris, although we are pretty much in agreement that Emmylou is no match for Joan from a quality-of-voice, sincerity-of-spirit standpoint. Emmylou is sweet, but distant. Good writers and good vocalists should be in your face.

After a while, maybe we're a hundred or so miles and at least one CD into a day, I may try to provide context to the trip or the music. Those first few days heading toward the AlCan, I directed my narration back in time to the Beatniks in the 1950s, and how Jack Kerouac's *On the Road* was truly an in-your-face experience—an extravaganza of literature and spontaneity, which inspired generations of nomadic wanderers, capturing the bone and sinew of the country in music and words. How Kerouac triggered an awakening of rebellious spirit—leading eventually to long hair, outrageous clothes, protests against racism and war. How this discontent was embraced by musicians we've been listening to, like Dylan, Joplin, even the Dead, whose "Truckin'" was rooted in the Kerouac *On the Road* message and mystique. I want Sam to see the connecting tissue in the arts—how music and travel can inspire great literature and how literature is in many ways like great music—both are by-products of new and incredible experiences—and how our own odyssey has been inspired by all of these ideas.

My take on cultural history may be skewed because of my prejudiced view of the impact of *On the Road*—a book that continues to exhilarate me after a dozen readings. I know that all Kerouac wanted to do was to write a great novel and to be recognized for his literary achievements, not unlike Bob Dylan, whose mission was to play classic folk music, recording and understanding elements of our culture and history; neither Kerouac nor Dylan aspired to world-changing motives or visions. But Kerouac is someone I can personally relate to and is a reasonable starting point to explain an age that is entirely foreign to Sam and the remarkable transition that took place in this country, producing an environment and an ethic that turned the country upside down, for good and bad, a condition that the Baby Boomers, me included, are handing over to our children now.

Kerouac wrote *On the Road* spontaneously, non-stop, in three weeks, on a roll of paper, sheets taped together so as not to interrupt his momentum. He was truckin', allowing his heart and his intellect to define and propel his quest for literary significance and spiritual relevance. As Dean Moriarty, the crazy, nomadic, sleazy, anti-hero character in the book, says, "You choose your own road in life. 'What's your road, man,' he says, 'Holybed road, madman road, rainbow road . . . it's an anywhere road for anybody, anyhow.'" But understand, I told Sam, it took Kerouac four years of thinking and suffering and failing and starting again to clear the way for his three weeks of brilliance. "Understand that brilliance may seem magical—it is magical, in a way—but it is the substance and the end product of a process. Picasso did not begin life with brilliance. The Dyl was a small-time Minnesota kid, who maybe had braces, just like you—dirty fingernails, pimply complexion. He did not begin life with brilliance. He worked toward it, tirelessly, until brilliance seemed to descend upon him."

Later, taking a break from Harry Potter, Sam and I will read Bob Dylan's *Chronicles*, his terrific memoir, and learn about the folk music scene he helped inspire in Greenwich Village in New York a little more than a decade after *On the Road*. We will also read Phil Lesh's autobiography—Lesh was the bass guitarist for The Dead and a founder of the group, along with Jerry Garcia—who will introduce Sam to Ken Kesey and the Merry Pranksters and the heady flower child days in San Francisco that turned on and tuned out so many young people. We'll rent the film *Easy Rider* and watch Dennis Hopper and Peter Fonda, cruising on their choppers in the deep south, blown up in the final few minutes of the film and then in the truck discuss (and debate) how they—Hopper and Fonda vs. their redneck killers—represented the lines of division and transformation in this country then and, to some extent, even now.

Truckin' was a word utilized in many songs, mostly blues, during the Depression era—mostly in the south. "Truckin' My Blues Away," by Blind Boy Fuller, was popular in Alabama, Mississippi, and Georgia in the early 1930s. "Truckin'" or "trucking" is also a dance, introduced at the Cotton Club in New York at about the same time, according to Bessie Jones in her book, *Step It Down*. Jones says that trucking is a two-step strut: "Step forward with the right foot, bring the left foot up to a close, step in place with the right foot, and rest. Repeat with the opposite feet." Jones warns readers to refer to trucking as "strutting" when discussing the dance with older folks because the word "truck" was also slang for sexual intercourse. So maybe the "F" word today is the equivalent to the "T" word in the south back then. The irony of intercourse is inescapable, we conclude. As my father had counseled me so many years ago: It's good to do—and bad to say it.

Wet Run

THE ALCAN WAS OUR second truckin 'trip. The first was the year before, 2003, when we bought the Ranger and wandered the lower 48, spontaneously, for a month. That year, we went, not necessarily in exact order, to:

Connecticut. This was to be the "dry run" for the Ranger, a test of comfort and mechanical soundness before heading west, but it rained relentlessly that week and the Ranger's rear window began to leak, soaking the floor of the truck, so we began referring to the Connecticut ride as our "wet run." The leak was never fixed. Wherever we wandered, when the rain came down, there was always a river in the Ranger.

New Jersey. We were checking on a house we owned near Atlantic City, where we had spent a great deal of time when Sam was younger. We liked running on the Boardwalk; Sam was beginning to weigh the possibility of running the entire Boardwalk and back, approximately twelve miles, nonstop. He would soon do this—an amazing achievement for a thirteen-year-old. A marathon, 26.2 miles, would be next.

Ohio. The Rock and Roll museum—to pay our respects to The Dead, The Stones, Bob Dylan ("The Dyl" to Sam), The Who—the folks who, along with Gary Paulsen, helped inspire our on the road experience, and journeyed with us, sharing the intimacy of the cab, coast to coast.

Washington, D.C. The Holocaust Museum, to pay homage to all of the Gutkinds murdered before and during the war. We watched movies of the captured Jews, directed by German soldiers at gunpoint, digging trenches in the ground. When the trenches were deep enough, the Jews were lined up in such a way that when the Germans fired their rifles, the Jews would fall into them, one by one, like dominoes. These silent movies were played over and over again—and Sam and I were amazed at how the prisoners hurried to their shovels to dig when the Germans ordered them. Why hurry? Why not cut and run? We imagined we could hear the dull thud of finality as the Jews, shot dead, toppled to the ground.

Missouri. The Jail Museum in Independence, where a "volunteer historian" with a thick red beard and a baseball cap shoved over his bushy, curly red-and-grayish hair explained that the building was built in 1901 to house chain gangs. The jail closed in 1933—and was resurrected in the early 1950s. Former President Harry Truman, an Independence resident, raised the first $1,000 for the renovation, but it was a challenge. "Most people thought he was feeding them a line when he called them up to ask for money and said, 'Hello, this is President Harry Truman speaking.'"

Down the road from Independence there was a wooden cigar-store Indian perched on the porch of a general store. The walls of the porch were decorated with hundreds of old license plates, rusted and battered, but representing, according to the man who greeted us, every state in the Union, except for Delaware. "I actually never met a Delawarean," he said. "Delaware is such a small state, people don't live there—they just pass through it." He offered to sell us coonskin caps with live coons inside the tail. "We also have beaver foot backscratchers." The man held up a claw, attached to a gnarled, rustic branch covered with shiny Shellac. "If you need a backscratcher, this is a good one."

"I don't think so," I said.

"Well then, you can use it as a soup ladle."

"How would that work?"

"If you've got uninvited guests and they come over for dinner and they see you use this for a soup ladle, they won't stay long."

The next stop was Amarillo, Texas, to see the Helium Centennial Time Columns: four stainless-steel time capsules, three on the bottom, coming together like a tripod, and a fourth intersecting in the middle and shooting straight up, six stories into the sky—a dramatic, erect penis–like shaft glittering in the relentless southwest Texas sun.

Most of our destinations that summer were spontaneous. We saw signs; or we were beckoned by winding lonely roads or intrigued by overheard conversations. But I *wanted* to visit Amarillo—it was a preferred destination—for it was "the site of my first real job as a writer," I explained to Sam. "Sort of a writer, anyway. I was a publicist," I confessed. Writers didn't go to college to learn to write, I explained—there were no creative writing degrees back then. Writers lived lives like real people working at menial jobs during the day, and they wrote at night in little garrets in New York in Greenwich Village or Paris or other romantic places. Amarillo didn't quite fit into the romantic place category, but it was my option out of Pittsburgh and pathway into a different working world.

The event I was hired to coordinate was devised to inaugurate and promote the Time Columns. It began when four helicopters hovered over the site and dropped a large black tarpaulin on top of the entire monument, thus concealing it from view. The corners of the tarpaulin were securely anchored. "The day before the official inauguration, dozens of large helium-filled weather balloons were attached to the tarp in dozens of places, end-to-end. Senators, congressmen, government bigwigs came from all across the country. The airport was mobbed. Every visitor was personally welcomed by the Amarillo Greeting Club: two rows of twelve cowboys in red gabardine pants, white shirts, blue bandanas, white gloves and hats, lined up like toy soldiers in front of the exit doors waiting to shake every visitor's hand and thank them for coming to Amarillo, which is what they said: "Welcome to Amarillo. Thanks for coming to Amarillo. Amarillo salutes you."

The inaugural ceremonies featured high school bands playing the national anthem, the state anthem, and "The Yellow Rose of Texas." TV cameras from the three networks were represented. At noon, cowboys stationed at the spots where the tarpaulin had been anchored to the balloons swung their axes. The ropes holding the tarpaulin down were severed. With music playing and cameras rolling, the balloons began rising, first slowly, but then ever faster, climbing higher into the sky, lifting the tarp majestically skyward. And thus the Helium Centennial Time Columns were dramatically revealed! The crowd hooted and hollered, then settled in for beer and barbecue, baked beans and Texas toast. "It was bizarre," I told Sam. "So much money and effort for such a lame idea."

But when Sam and I arrived at the monument, I was surprised to see how striking the Time Columns were—tall and majestic, soaring up out of the flat, sandy, red Texas terrain. And the location was not where I remembered it to be, which was in a blighted area of the city. I later learned that the Columns were actually airlifted by helicopters to the Don Harrington Discovery Center, Amarillo's science museum—and it seemed to fit into the grounds quite perfectly there, as if it designed for that spot from the beginning. I was suddenly proud of the work I had done, even though it lacked literary merit, but also, just as suddenly and also surprisingly, disappointed. The plaque that contained the names of all the people who played a major role in helping the monument become a reality was missing me!

In some ways I guess I didn't actually care if I was given credit or not—I don't live in Amarillo and I am not a scientist or engineer. But after I had told Sam that I was one of the prime movers, to not be listed on the plaque was embarrassing. I don't want my son to think me a liar—or even an overzealous exaggerator (even if that is true), especially in this situation in which I did in fact have a great deal to do with making the event and the monument a reality.

But I had a bigger and better monument in mind as we headed northwest from Amarillo: Monument Valley, where the director John Ford made all of those old dramatic black and white westerns like *The Searchers* and *Stagecoach*. I remembered, when I was there before on my motorcycle, finding a road, partially unpaved and incredibly bumpy, that went up close to the mountains and the awesome rock formations that seemed like majestic sculptures, more remarkable and awe-inspiring that than anything ever conceivably man-made. For a long time Sam and I could not find this road—we didn't even know where to look. I couldn't remember how I had gotten to it before—I had just stumbled on it. I was just about ready to give up—we were actually headed out of and away from the valley on tiny winding Highway 163 after driving north from the Arizona/Utah state line—when we saw an old, soiled, sign with partially faded letters that read, "Valley of the Gods."

That sign must have been very old because, for sure, there were a couple of points on the road where our Ranger, in all of its four-wheel-drive glory, could barely make it. In the entire seventeen miles we only passed two other vehicles, both going in the opposite direction. But we were blown away by the hulking magnificent images, skyscraper-tall, that filled the skyline in every direction, rising more than a thousand feet from the desert floor. We met an old Indian lady sitting alone near the Totem Pole monument, a Navajo, who referred to the area as Tse Bii' Ndzisgalii, which I later learned means "Valley of the Rocks." In the Navajo way, the old woman never looked at our faces; as she talked with us, she seemed to stare mystically, clear-eyed, into the landscape of her past.

That year we also went to Oklahoma City, where we visited the National Memorial—the site of Timothy McVeigh's bombed out Alfred P. Murrah Building. The monument was most impressive, with nine rows of 168 high, straight-backed chairs carved in black granite—material salvaged from the rubble of the building—and lined up, as in an empty church, where parishioners, represented in marble, might have been sitting—had they lived. Each person's chair is positioned in the row that corresponds to the floor on which they worked or were visiting. The five westernmost chairs honor those who were killed outside the building.

WE COME HERE TO REMEMBER THOSE WHO WERE KILLED THOSE WHO SURVIVED, AND THOSE WHO CHANGED FOREVER. MAY ALL WHO LEAVE HERE KNOW THE IMPACT OF VIOLENCE AND HATRED.

Those words are carved into the granite and marble wall towering above a glittering reflecting pool in the middle of the compound. Here visitors dipped their hands in the water and pressed them against a copper and brass sculpture, hot from the beating rays of the sun, in order to feel more bonded with the victims and their survivors.

We also went to the Living Bible Museum. "You have," the woman at the front desk explained, "a choice of four self-guided Bible Walks." We chose Christian Martyrs—men who willingly gave their life to Jesus Christ. We walked through a room of dioramas, forty-one in all, with life-size wax figures in large, brightly illuminated display cases in a cavernous room in the pitch black darkness, accompanied by inspirational muzak. The wax figures in the display cases were not necessarily totally life-like and animated, but they were strangely compelling. The darkness made the experience feel kind of holy.

At the end of this show, we returned to the front desk and told the woman how much we appreciated the quiet intimacy of the museum. As I grow older, I find these evangelistic experiences thought-provoking. I am fascinated by the intensity of belief—no latitude for discussion, analysis, or debate. Sam, on the other hand, seems to be growing increasingly impatient with religious belief and its reliance on faith rather than scientific proof or, at the very least, any semblance of logic. His impatience with structured religious dogma will grow more intense as he gets older.

"I am so glad you enjoyed it," the woman said. "We want our facility to give solace—and inspire."

"Before we leave," I asked her then, "do you have a bathroom?"

"Right around the corner." Then she added, "We have running water, too."

"Well, that's a good thing," I commented.

"Not like in Biblical times," she replied.

The Jack London
of Rock and Roll

THE STORM EXPLODED over our Tundra with a cascading and relentless fury. Lightning lit up the sky in jagged electric yellow, like a great, cosmic camera flash, briefly thrusting the landscape into full illumination before plunging it back into a darkness as impenetrable as India ink. Seconds later, the accompanying thunder collided with our truck as if someone was inside our cab whaling on a bass drum.

For a moment, I tried to continue our conversation in order to keep Sam engaged and to not let on that I was no longer completely in control of the Tundra, which was lurching from side to side in the Alcan storm. But this was futile. I could not seem to concentrate on anything at that moment except the pain in my fingers as I squeezed the steering wheel and the pressure on my jaw as I clamped my teeth together, as if such exertion could force the wild wind and rain to cease their relentless battering.

I considered pulling over and waiting out the fury, but there was no shoulder wide enough to accommodate us—and no guardrail. A car or truck or one of the dozens of RVs on this road could plow into us because we would be sticking out too much. So I had no choice but to continue to push forward. If we did not keep up our momentum then the battering wind could just blow us off the road. We'd slip off the steep, muddy embankment and down over the side of the mountains, plunging seven thousand feet into the dark and inky emptiness. What had we proclaimed with exhilaration in conversation just a few minutes ago? We had been comparing the Rolling Stones and The Mick (Sam's nickname for Mick Jagger) to Alaska—raunchy and insanely erotic.

"The Mick's got an aura, a rare charisma most of us will never achieve," I told Sam.

"The Mick wails," Sam said. "Like Alaska. The Mick is primitive."

"Exactly, Sam!" I shrieked. "The Mick is the Jack London of rock and roll—he's music's 'Call of the wild.'"

I remember those last words, but I am not sure that Sam ever heard them because at that moment the rain and wind descended suddenly upon us in a jarring transformation from quiet conversation to raging turmoil. Comparing The Mick to Jack London was a fitting metaphor, but now, in this harrowing cacophony of nature unleashed, I feared that Sam would never hear it and I would never write it and that it really didn't matter one way or another because Sam and I could end up dead.

ONCE, MANY YEARS AGO, while traveling cross-country on my motorcycle with my friend, Burt, we were engulfed in a fierce storm in Yellowstone National Park, six or eight icy inches of snow on unplowed roads—in the middle of July. I knew it was foolhardy and dangerous to try to navigate the snow on two wheels. I could die—or be maimed—or be responsible for causing harm to other people as I skittered around in the blinding whiteness, but I felt trapped. There was nowhere to wait out the storm—no shelter, fire, food, or water. So we pushed forward. I can remember every detail:

I was leading and the snow was getting ever deeper and more treacherous, yet I rode progressively faster as we wound up and down the mountains. I watched the road ahead, fascinated by the way my front tire cut a narrow black line in the white powder, like a crayon in cotton. The harder the snow came, the faster I pressed along the highway. The sheets of snow caked on my face shield. I rode with one hand and gloved the shield with the other—back and forth—like a car's windshield wipers, pushing away the snow to see, seeing to go ever faster. I rode the white line, squeezing between the cars that were ahead, and the cars that came toward me from the opposite lane. Burt was somewhere behind, although I could not see through the ice that froze away his reflection in my rearview mirror.

At one point, we stopped at an outhouse, an old shack sagging under the weight of the snow. Burt pulled in beside me, but we didn't talk. We walked down the hill from the road toward the building, went inside, took off our shirts and rung them out. We smoked cigarettes, inhaling the foulness of the outhouse, trembling in the cold corner of the hut, laughing as if we were crazed. Later, plunging into the Tetons, the snow dissolved to rain. The roads were black and shiny, spiraling up and down the mountains. Forgetting caution, we ran from the cold, searching for the sun, leaning drunkenly into semi-circular bends, when Burt lost control and dumped head-on into the side of a rocky hill.

I heard the metal of Burt's machine scrape against the asphalt. In my rearview mirror, I saw the bike, with Burt riding the side of it, shooting a stream of golden sparks along the asphalt, smashing against a wall of rocks against a hill. Then I dropped my bike. I was running before the bike hit the ground. It caught my leg and I went down. I scrambled up and fell down again. I pawed at the ground until I pulled my leg out. Burt was wedged between the rocks and his machine and he was bleeding. The road had ripped through his rain suit and the Levi's under them, and scraped away his skin. He was covered with mud, and there were cinders stuck in the flesh of his leg.

"What happened?"

"I don't know. I think I got too tired. Maybe I went to sleep. I don't know. I can't remember anything about it right now."

We moved on for a few days, but the trip was over. Burt's bike was not in good shape and neither was he; his leg was bruised and battered. The fingers of my left hand were partially frostbitten. I could maneuver the motorcycle, but without the feel of the controls it did not seem the same. Looking back, it had been an adventure, exciting and dramatic—an elating experience even with the abrupt ending. Satisfying in many ways for a different drummer like me.

But I had no children then—I was alone. If I died, my parents would mourn me, my friends and relatives would miss me, maybe my death could be considered "legendary"—a rebel writer seeking truth and enlightenment on the road on two wheels. The brilliant novelist John Gardner died in a motorcycle accident a few days before he was to be married. The great British soldier T. E. Lawrence, played by Peter O'Toole in the movie *Lawrence of Arabia*, died in a motorcycle accident. But Gardner and Lawrence did nothing foolish to precipitate their deaths, save for riding motorcycles in the first place—and also drinking too much.

In the motorcycle movie *Easy Rider*, Peter Fonda and Dennis Hopper are assassinated by rednecks somewhere in Louisiana. The Hopper character triggers his own demise by giving the finger to two toothless backwoods thugs in a pick-up truck with a shotgun in a rear window rack—and they shoot him off his bike, reducing him to pieces, like a clay pigeon. Perhaps they would have shot him anyway, but surely, logically speaking, you don't flip the bird to a toothless moron aiming a shotgun at your eyeballs in backwoods Louisiana, unless you realize your fate and future are up for grabs. Hopper's cavalier reaction also gets Peter Fonda killed: the rednecks aren't stupid enough to leave a babbling witness.

So, okay, *Easy Rider* is not true, literally. But fiction is a mirror of reality—the characters and the venues in movies and books may be acts of imagination, but the essence and anchor of legitimacy is valid. How many good kids, black and white, heterosexual and homosexual, homeboys and northerners, were killed in the south during the last century by redneck radicals who tried to obliterate anything different and threatening to their privileged way of life? Hopper caused his own demise and that of his friend and partner—was I, similarly, on this rain-drenched road in northern Canada, flipping the bird at myself—at God—taunting fate?

Why had I been so foolish as to even think that truckin' the AlCan was a dramatic, romantic, thing to do? Because the spirit of Jack Kerouac's *On the Road* had electrified me and boiled in my bloodstream since my senior year of high school? Because *Easy Rider,* with its thundering, haunting, intoxicating road music from The Byrds, Jimi Hendrix, Steppenwolf, and The Band, screamed and echoed in my brain? Because I wanted to plant a seed of my on-the-road obsession in my son Sam? Because I was relentlessly searching for my lost youth, trying to shape my legacy, trying to accumulate memories to savor when I am too old to do anything else? I can't help but ask myself the question as the wind and rain turns our Tundra into tumbleweed: am I acting my age—or am I trying to be someone I am not? Am I an older dad trying to act like a younger dad just for the sake of my own ego and satisfaction? To show my contemporaries that although I was way behind them in the parenthood role, that I know how to do it best? To show my own father that his son could be what he was not?

My own father was out of touch; so many fathers are out of touch, out of synch, uninspired, frustrated and enraged and not engaged. But I know that what I am doing now could be worse.

All of these doubts and recriminations were racing through my mind as I battled the avalanching, unceasing, wind-ripped downpour on the AlCan. Lightning and thunder exploded in blinding tremors. At one point, I saw a bear looming in front of us in the middle of the road, its furry chunk of a head and shiny black snout illuminated in the slash of my headlights.

I blinked once and then again. "Well holy shit," I said aloud. "That bear is drinking a glass of wine!"

I swerved at the sight of the bear, felt the rear tires skidding out of control, and imagined that we would fishtail off the road and slide over the embankment. When I regained control seconds later, I realized that the bear had been a mirage, precipitated by a previous conversation with a strange woman in a restaurant called Buckshot Bette's—and a response to the stress of grappling so long with this endless storm.

"A bear stuck his head in my car window," she had said.

"You were sitting in your car out in the middle of the woods?"

"I was sleeping with the window open so that I could breathe in the night air, and there was an empty wine bottle in the seat next to me which I had finished off the night before. I think he wanted to drink some of it. Bears get stressed out, too."

Maybe bears, but not Sam. That night, I looked over at Sam as the storm lashed its relentless fury down upon us and I battled the twisting steering wheel and the blind blackness of the road. He was staring into the windshield watching as the wipers fought a futile contest against the downpour as if he could actually see into the inky blankness. He didn't seem to notice when the thunder crashed repeatedly and the Tundra shook like a baby rattle, as if it we were about to shatter into pieces. He smiled as I cursed each element—the night, the rain, and the wind—shouting my favorite "F" words at the top of my lungs, smashing my fist on the dashboard with pent up frustration. "Sam, I am going crazy—this is crazy!" I confessed.

"This is fun," Sam said.

From Sam's Journal:

And then, in the evening, we hit a thunderstorm. We had been through these quick storms before—but there were none like this that we had experienced. We had seen the clouds from far away. After a while, they were still there. Usually in one of the flash interval storms, we see the clouds, in a half hour it begins to rain, and then it stops. But here, we had been seeing them become progressively darker for about an hour to an hour and a half, but we still did not consider this significant. Then it looked very bad—gray clouds all around. Suddenly, it began to rain. The wind was intense—it began to blow on our truck. We began shaking side to side.

Hello?

I WOKE UP AT five o'clock with the sun was shining through the curtains. I pushed my way out of bed, got myself dressed, and went outside. By five-thirty, the sun was bright and the chill in the air was clean and refreshing. The parking lot was filled with trucks, mostly mud covered, like our Toyota Tundra—brown, battered vehicles, survivors, like us, of the many AlCan storms.

This valley was surrounded by thick tree-covered hillsides. Most of the buildings were new; even the oldest buildings were not as old as I am. This was the North American frontier as I have never seen it nor will probably ever see again. We had stumbled in here—a single yellow light, like a lighthouse in a storm, that I had been following through the rain and wind for more than an hour.

There aren't a lot of towns on the AlCan—it is pretty much the way it was when it was carved out of the wilderness seventy years ago. Angling northwest for nearly fifteen hundred miles, the AlCan stretches from Dawson Creek, British, Columbia, through the Yukon Territory, to Delta Junction, Alaska, about a hundred miles southeast of Fairbanks. Primitive compared to the superhighways in the lower 48, the AlCan is gradually becoming more navigable. People who regularly travel it say it's no longer a wilderness road; rather, it's a road through the wilderness.

The AlCan was completed in nine months by the U.S. Army, an idea proposed in 1930 but not acted upon until after Pearl Harbor, when the Japanese invaded the Aleutian Islands, near the westernmost tip of Alaska. President Franklin Delano Roosevelt began to fear an overland incursion and launched the AlCan project in early 1942. The AlCan made it possible to transport thousands of troops and warplanes to repel an invasion.

About every fifty miles on the road, there's usually a waypoint—a spark of civilization. We pulled into this particular outpost last night at about midnight. They had a room for us and we could get some food. Sam was hungry and tired; I was shaken and exhausted, but relieved. The storm had been persistent, pursuing us like an assassin on the hunt, banging our Tundra relentlessly. A good night's sleep enhanced my feelings of relief at having fought our way through the storm—and not panicking or dying in the process.

There was a special feel to this place, I realized, as I walked into the sunlight, a chill of excitement and newness as I wandered through the parking lot, even this early in the morning. Everyone shared an edge of enthusiasm and friendliness. Strolling aimlessly, I passed an attractive woman coming out of a restaurant, one of the few women we'd seen in this mostly masculine atmosphere. "Sunlight and springtime," she said, with awe in her voice. "This is a wonderful switch from all those months of grayness. And no rain," she added. "I am so thankful."

A tall handsome young man, yellow-haired, was fixing the sidewalk in front of the hotel, wearing a T-shirt proclaiming "Australian Athletic." I didn't know what that meant, exactly, but it seemed fitting to combine the northern Canadian Rocky Mountain experience with the rugged, youthful vitality of Australia. I loved those words: Youthful. Vital. I remember so clearly the days when I could use them to describe me.

ON THIS TRIP I have read the end of Phillip Roth's *American Pastoral*, a book I started nearly a year ago but was only just now finishing. A wonderful book, although I had to go back to the beginning after I finished to figure out how it started and how the story at the end, which I been reading the past week, connected to the story I had read in the beginning, a year ago, and which had initially attracted me. I had forgotten that Roth had started with himself, or Nathan Zuckerman, as the narrator, with strong memories of the character Swede, Seymour Levov, and how the narration slowly transitioned from Zuckerman to the Swede, never to return to the original narrator, Zuckerman. Roth won the National Book Critics Circle award for the book.

But then with the book complete, I started a second Roth, *The Counterlife*, which begins with the dentist Henry Zuckerman, who suffers from a heart problem that requires him to take beta blockers and hypertensive medications. This, in turn, eventually interferes with his ability to get an erection, and the lack of a sex drive slowly begins to work on him until, driven mad by his inability to have sex with his eager, willing nurse, Wendy, he submits to dangerous open-heart surgery, which, he hopes, will alleviate the need for medication.

In this narrative, Roth eventually plays two tricks, one on the reader and another on me, personally. First, the narrator, Henry, gradually becomes his older brother, Nathan, the same Nathan who had started the *American Pastoral* narration and disappeared, and from whom Henry had been estranged and had tried to contact as a last desperate attempt to wrench him back from insanity. Second, I too had been taking medicine for hypertension, but I should have been taking medicine for paranoia. Reading Roth, I was beginning to suspect that something was happening to my own sexual functioning because, when I read that section of the book on the AlCan Highway, where men are real men and exceedingly virile, like "Australian Athletic," I could not remember my last erection.

BESIDE ME AT A TABLE is an older man, clearly in his fifties, perhaps older—perhaps even older than me. You can tell he is old by the way he chews, working his jaw up and down methodically, his pointed chin like a threshing machine; his teeth aren't his own.

But he is with a young woman, in her late twenties or early thirties. You can tell this by listening to her voice, still ringing with the clarity of youth, and I think for a while, as I watch them, that she is his daughter. But I begin to suspect that she is something else, more than a daughter, because of the comfortable way they are with one another. He is smiling and speaking softly to her and she is smiling back, kindly. They are German tourists. She seems to have a wedding band on. He is dressed very traditionally, sweater and shirt, in the conservative manner of a man his age, and she is in Levi's and a Levi's jacket, much like me. She eats a bowl of cornflakes smothered in yogurt, then another bowl. They eat very slowly. They eat quite a lot. Getting up from the table and going to the buffet for more, back and forth, until, during one of these excursions, he leans forward over the yogurt and cornflakes and kisses her passionately. I hear the smack of his lips. She responds.

This is something I have seen more often in Europe. In the United States there are gay couples and mixed-race couples here and there, but old men and young women seem almost nonexistent. The barista at the Starbucks near my house in Pittsburgh, the pretty, thin, tall woman who often works mornings, once said, smiling over at Sam, "Is he your grandson?"

I replied, annoyed, "Why couldn't he be my son?"

Later in the day, the barista apologized to me, saying that I was right to be annoyed; these days everyone has to be so careful to be politically correct, she says.

I am not sure that that was a real apology, but I too was sorry I spoke out.

RECENTLY, I WAS ON A cross-trainer, an aerobic machine for legs and arms, at my health club, in the final ten minutes of a one-hour computerized circuit. I was talking with my friend Susan. We were both philosophical, discussing forgetfulness and our attempts to keep our short-term memories intact. This is the difficult challenge of middle age—remembering day-to-day details. Like people you see suddenly on the street or at the movies that make you freeze in embarrassment because you can't connect names with their faces. You know you know them. But how? When?

Not long ago, I slammed face first into a plate glass door when I was trying to make a quick and invisible exit from a meeting. The impact pushed my new Armani glasses into my face and ripped the skin on the bridge of my nose. Blood poured down my cheeks as I bolted from the building. I was angry for not looking where I was going—and mortified—and I immediately blamed it on my diminishing capacity to stay alert due to my never-ending, relentlessly advancing, inevitable descent into old age.

This feeling of advancing age is endemic, a haunting bad dream, and an incurable disease that gradually engulfs and destroys. Middle age is like having a black widow spider creeping up your body from your ankles to your neck. Every day when I crawl out of bed, my muscles and joints screaming with resistance and soreness, I can feel the spider coming closer to my jugular vein, its presence more prevalent, inevitable and unwavering, ready to bite and to suck the life out me, painfully, torturously.

All I can do, in defense, is to run faster and longer, beating my body into submission, whether training for marathon running with Sam or expending every ounce of my energy lifting weights and working out at the health club—where I was finishing, now, drenched with perspiration and exhaustion. Sixty-five minutes, 962 calories at level 15. I got off my cross-trainer after the cool-down, wiped my face with a towel, and put on my coat, catching my breath and continuing my conversation with Susan.

"Sometimes I space out," Susan said.

"I work really hard to keep things together," I told her. "I'm constantly monitoring myself. I feel the pressure. I'm always fighting to focus. I don't want Sam to see—or to think for a moment—that I'm slipping."

As I headed to the door, I checked for my wallet, car keys, water bottle, gloves, making sure not to forget anything. But then I realized I couldn't find my cell phone. I searched the front pouch of my nylon jacket, where I normally keep it, and then the side pockets—I even checked the bands of my socks. I went back to the cross-trainer. Two weeks before this event, I had driven all the way home from this club and showered before I realized my phone was missing. I searched everywhere before retracing my steps back to the club. I finally found it where I had initially put it—in the cup holder of the cross trainer. I didn't usually answer when I got a call while exercising, but I monitor the caller ID.

But today the phone wasn't in the cup holder, either. I stood, just for an instant, in the middle of the club, surrounded by dozens of aerobic and weight-lifting machines, men in sweats, women in Spandex, feeling a slight edge of panic welling up inside, while sympathizing with Susan as she rambled on about her own middle-aged difficulties, when I realized, suddenly, that the phone I was now so desperately seeking was in my hand, against my ear, the vehicle through which I was talking.

Sam's Journal, 2005:

I have been looking at the games at AddictingGames.com lately, looking at some software, and looking at what people like. I realize that making a game popular is certainly different from making a game good. I think good games involve more thought, and are more realistic (or have a real, complex motive/strategy). One of the reasons the games at AddictingGames.com are so popular is because they are free. But also because they spread extremely well by word of mouth. More complex games are reviewed and rated by magazines like PC Gamer. People follow these magazines, and that is good. In moderation.

One thing about games is they generally cover a small area of ideas. They are usually about one thing. So they are usually better when kept more diverse—they cover a broader spectrum of ideas, preventing you from getting bored of one idea. I stay on one game usually from about two to six weeks. I want one game that stays interesting and replayable. Replayable not just meaning that it changes the game world, but that it remains interesting and full of information. Is Civilization IV the answer? The "tech tree" can change each game. So the game strategy changes, as well as the world, and the opponent.

So I have to ask: what is it in people that allows some players to still consider a game (like online RISK) interesting after playing it with little new information on the same or similar map 1,437 times?

Some entertainment industries do not suffer from this so much. A game is confined to what is programmed with information. Movies, books, and other things have so many possibilities that they can always stay interesting. They are about life. Life is more complex than any one person can know or discover, probably. So it stays filled with new things. I will now prevent a philosophical conflict with something stated in a previous entry: a single movie or book is not replayable—the multitude of them are. They allow for more diversity.

Artful Charlie

WE SEE A SIGN, one of my favorite backcountry signs, a short and sweet message that says it all, quite succinctly: EAT! And, since that is exactly what we intend to do, we take the bait. Down a road maybe a quarter-mile, nothing happens—no town, no "Eat!"

Following a sign that goes nowhere—at least nowhere quickly—is a periodic on-the-road annoyance. Signs remain, untended, withered and faded by weather, long after the object of the signs have disappeared. I am about to turn around, but Sam says, "Keep going, Dad. I'm really hungry." It's hard to know when to schedule meals for Sam. He is not hungry, not hungry, not hungry—no matter how many times you ask him, Sam is not hungry—and then, suddenly, out of the blue, Sam is starving, and getting food fast becomes a crisis, a life-and-death situation. We weren't at that point yet, but I could see hunger welling up in his eyes.

"There's nothing here, Sam," I say. "It's a false positive."

Sam laughs. "It promises, but does not deliver."

But now here's a row of buildings, mostly vacant, and an old main street. There are a couple of old cars in the front yards of plain clapboard houses—homemade "for sale" signs in the windshields. I see a woman sitting on her steps, watching the traffic and, since she is watching us, I pull over to ask about the source of the "EAT!"

Traveling the country on both two and four wheels, I have learned that it is usually better to ask women for directions than men. Women, generally, are friendlier, more articulate, and, most important, more honest. Men like to think that they always know where they are going, so they give you directions whether they are sure of them or not. It's a king-of-the-hill thing. Men tell you which way to go and then, as you pull away, you can almost imagine them beating their fists against their chests—triumphing over a less virile (or knowledgeable) man.

The woman immediately directed us to a diner, the source of the EAT!—which looked just like Ritter's, our Pittsburgh breakfast haunt.

The people in the booth behind us, one woman and two men, are clean-cut and articulate, not your typical homey country folk, yet they are discussing court appearances, jail time, and restraining orders. We listen. The woman is especially vocal—and lovely. Slender, blonde, and fragile-looking, hardly the jailbird-type, although she says, laughing, "I stabbed my boyfriend with a fork. He bled like a pig."

"You can never tell by looking at people who they are inside and what they might do at any given time," I tell Sam. "Looks are deceiving. You have to always be careful."

"Then why do you want me to talk with people I don't know," he asks, "or take videos of them?"

"It's for the experience. That's how you learn about other people—by taking chances sometimes and engaging."

"How do you know they're not dangerous or they won't annoy you and put you in a bad mood for the rest of the day?"

"There aren't that many people who will want to stab you with a fork," I said.

"I just don't like it when people come up and talk with me," Sam said. "I like privacy."

"Even when they offer you money?" I ask.

WHEN SAM WAS SIX or seven and began to live with me full-time, we started to come to Ritter's for breakfast, and immediately, Charlie, the old, fat short-order cook, began creating for Sam pancake sculptures.

At first, Charlie created storybook or cartoon characters or TV personalities, like Barney or Bart Simpson, pouring out the rich yellow batter and shaping it carefully with spoon and spatula on the hot sizzling griddle. Charlie was also holiday-oriented. He produced sculptures of pumpkins for Halloween, hearts for Valentine's Day, Christmas trees and ornaments, sleds and Santas. Snowmen in winter; sunsets in summer—all shaped artfully from golden-brown batter with kitchen accoutrements, like raisins, chocolate chips, twisted crusts of toast.

Charlie also tailored his creations to Sam's special interests: The Milky Way during Sam's celestial phase, Nike shoes when we started running, boats, anchors, beach umbrellas the weeks before we took off for our summer home on the Jersey shore. A pancake computer was served on three plates, with a pancake monitor on one, a pancake keyboard (with chocolate chips for keys) on another, and a pancake mouse on the third, connected artfully to the keyboard with strips of bacon.

We sit at the counter at Ritter's on stools in front of where Charlie cooks so that we can see him throw the breakfast plates crammed with home fries, bacon, or sausage on the stainless steel counter with a spin and a yell: "Rosa! Mandy! Jackie! You're up!" Or when the plates sit there under the warming lights for too long: "Bobbie, where the hell are you? Bobbie?"

Charlie directs the waitresses about the proper way to serve his pancake sculptures, for frequently the waitresses turn his creations upside down or sideways when presenting to Sam. Then, traditionally, there's always the obligatory moment of silence when Sam and I and the waitress look at Charlie's masterpiece and try to guess what it is.

Charlie's ideas for pancake sculptures can be off the wall. Like a large circle with a hole in the middle. We thought it was a donut, but he had actually created the Grand Canyon. This was the week before we were to start truckin'. We were once served two flat disks, round and fluffy and brown, and this time we had no idea. We guessed and guessed. "Alright, what is it?" we asked.

Charlie has come around the counter from behind the grill to serve us personally. "It's pancakes the way everybody else gets them!" he says, whooping and laughing. Charlie laughs too loudly and much too long. And he puts his face right into your face when he laughs. Charlie only has two or three teeth, and they are both yellow and pointy, so you look deep down into the red cavern of his mouth, a smile pasted on your frozen face, waiting for him to be called back to the kitchen before your lips fall off or your face self destructs.

Sam always appreciated Charlie's efforts, as long as those objets d'art did not interfere with or in any way alter the food he was being served. The fact that Sam wants exactly the same breakfast every morning, with no variations, is just the way Sam is—he doesn't like change. This intrigued one of the morning Ritter's regulars, Gloria, who one day went up to Sam and said, "I'll give you twenty dollars if you change what you're going to eat today."

Most of the time, the people who approach Sam, unlike Gloria, ask what grade he is in, what school he goes to, or how old he is. I can see Sam brace himself for the inevitable question every time I introduce him to someone new. He and I know that the people who ask him these questions are trying to be friendly and nice, but can't they understand how bored he must be telling people day after day what grade he is in or how tall he is?

One day, Pete, one of the three Greek brothers who own Ritter's, asked Sam if he wants Charlie to stop making the crazy pancake sculptures for his breakfast. "Maybe you are getting too old for this," Pete adds. But Sam is so taken aback by Pete's question that he is too dumbfounded to answer. It is inconceivable to Sam that there would come a day when Sam and I would not be going to Ritter's every morning and Charlie would not be designing an elaborate work of art out of pancake batter for him to pass judgment on—which was why Gloria's offer of money to make a change did not for an instant tempt him. Sam turned down the twenty dollars without a pause or a blink.

I looked at Sam's face as Gloria stood there, leaning over his shoulders and slowly pulling greenbacks out of her wallet to tempt him. "Fifty dollars?" she says.

Sam still wouldn't do it—maybe not even for a hundred dollars, although quite recently when I reminded him of the incident—we still go to Ritter's from time-to-time, although the pancake sculptures are a part of the past—he said he would gladly sell out his breakfast options today for the right price. Sam is maturing.

NEAR THE "EAT" DINER we met two men in T-shirts, gritty guys from Alabama, unshaven, drenched in the pouring rain, lashing down an old Subaru Sambar—a tiny crab-like mini-truck, which, they say, has the lowest deck body—closest to the ground—and the roomiest cargo bed, comparatively, of any truck ever made. There are only fifty Subaru Sambars in the nation, the two men say, the rain pelting down on us as we talk, and though the Sambars seem odd and impractical— they won't hold much cargo—they are legal to drive. "Someday they'll be worth a fortune"—they beam and space the word out, their yellow, tobacco-stained teeth protruding from dirty wet whiskers—"*fortshuuu-uun,*" like it's a prayer. "We'll sell 'em online to stock brokers in New York and actors from Hollywood. Rich folks who want to show off their money and prove that they're cool. No one is dumb enough to buy a Sambar in Alabama," they chuckle, "except us."

Not to forget the man and woman with a little Nash Metropolitan convertible with a Continental chrome wheel on the back, broken down on the side of the road. The Metropolitan is yellow on the outside, yellow leather seats and dashboard in the inside, with a classic wooden steering wheel.

The woman runs a small pudgy hand, fingernails glistening with bright red polish, through her matted gray hair and turns to her husband, who has been partially concealed, ducking down behind the open hood of the car and peering inside. The husband, George, is wearing sunglasses and a powder-blue shirt, buttoned up at the neck. He has bright yellow suspenders to match the color of the car.

"We bought this here car, actually, in 1979," he says.

"Sight unseen," the woman, whose name is Loretta, adds.

"Do you collect Metropolitans?"

"We own twenty-four Metropolitans at the moment. We have a '54 that's unique. The guy we bought it from cut a hole in the back and put a trunk in it cause they didn't have trunks in Metropolitans until 1957," Loretta says.

"We got a cute pink-and-white hardtop 1957, with a right-hand driver, that's from England, and a black-and-white hardtop, 1958, with 873,000 miles on it."

"Actually, we don't got that anymore," says Loretta.

"A gal bought it from us finally," says George, "That's right. Did it all through e-mail, the whole negotiation and sale."

"And her only stipulation?" Loretta asks.

George and Loretta look at each other and laugh; they are having a great time talking about themselves and their beloved Metropolitans, even though they are stranded in the middle of nowhere.

"Her golf clubs had to fit into the back," George says.

"She brought her golf bag when she came to pick up the car," says Loretta. "Put them in the back seat, saw they were safe and snug, gave us the check, and drove away, car and clubs and all."

"People are funny," says George.

"Everyone got their obsessions," says Loretta.

"Your obsession?" I say to Sam later, back on the road. "It's computers, right?

"I guess," says Sam. "Programming, gaming." He thinks for a while. "This summer it's music and truckin'," he adds. "What's your obsession, Dad?"

"Guess," I tell him. "In fact, you don't have to guess—you know."

"Yes," he says, "I think I know." We pause and glance at one another. "It's Sam, isn't it?"

"Yes, although I am not sure 'obsession' is a fair way to describe it. I am not obsessed; I am, rather constantly concerned and engaged." Sam smiles. "You think obsessions are unhealthy?" I ask

"They could be. A person can take an obsession too far."

SAM TOOK HIS computer with him every year we were on the road, except for the first year. He was deeply involved in gaming then, although his obsessions have evolved, significantly, as we will discover later. In 2005, traveling in the Tundra, he added this entry to his journal:

Now, several times, I have played on my Nintendo DS, on the road. I have, on this trip, almost exclusively been playing a game called Grand Theft Auto, for the Game Boy Advance. I have noticed that, even with its Mafia theme, it is extremely violent, allowing you to kill random people on the street indiscriminately, carjack cars, and do other violent but admittedly fun things. For example, you can carjack a police car and go around on a "vigilante" mission arresting people and receiving money from the police. Steal an ambulance, and get paid taking people to the hospital. Or take a taxi, and do just that.

I wonder why people are so afraid of games like that: they are only games—that is clear, and it is not difficult to distinguish between the game and reality. In the game, people you kill usually do not have names, and the police take bribes. When you are arrested, you bribe the police. You lose $1000 and then are back out on the street. Or if you are "wasted," you end up at the hospital, again losing $1000, this time for medical fees. But it is clearly a game, and I admittedly have trouble understanding how people could get the game confused with or even seriously relate it to reality. The game provides a refuge—it is a constant source of entertainment, anywhere, always presenting a challenge. No wonder the video game market is so important. What are people interested in, and what makes certain games profitable, while others are not.

These are questions to ask myself since I have plans to start a business with my friend from St. Edmund's Academy, Jack Billings, and one thing we plan to develop is video games. I know it is a competitive market, but, with a website, I hope we can get our games out relatively easily, and begin to accumulate some money. I think we can do it—it is something I am very interested in. And Jack Billings seems relatively interested as well. I am not sure what his end motivations are—he once told me his dream is to "unify the world," but I am not sure what this all means.

The Dyl

As WE BARRELED through Alberta, Saskatchewan, and the Yukon Territory, the furious and unpredictable weather never stopped—rain, snow, sleet, hail, pelted down upon us as we snaked up this winding two-lane road connecting the many jagged peaks of the Canadian Rockies, the names of which I had been forced to memorize in high school, useless, save for competition in that old game, "Geography," in which a geographical point (city, country, body of water, etc.) initiated by one player obligates the next player to say the name of a geographical point beginning with the letter of the last letter of the name stated before it: thus, Moose Jaw leads to Winnipeg which segues to Green River and then to Regina (pronounced with a long "I"). The game goes on and on, leapfrogging around the world, until a participant is stumped.

Last night at a gasoline station at Pink Mountain, mile 143 on the AlCan, in northern British Columbia, the man filling our tank in the pouring rain pointed at the glow of sun in the distant sky and said, "Just look at that. I been here all my life, but I can never get over all of that gorgeousness."

"Yes," I said. "The colors are striking."

"The sky actually glows a deep pink on clear mornings during sunrise because it reflects down on our fireweed blossoms."

"It doesn't look too pink, now."

"This rain blots the colors, but it's going to stop sooner or later."

"Why Pink Mountain?"

"Go on up the road for ten miles or so to Lilly Lake, Moose Lick Creek, or Halfway River," he said. "Take a look back at the mountain then and see if we're pink. We might be—although, like I said, the rain ruins the view."

"It fools me," I said. "All day the weather has been toying with us. I see the sun in the distance and I think the rain will stop any minute, and it does stop for while, but then it comes back worse than ever."

"It comes back again and again," he interrupted. "The damn wind forces it back so that the same storm rains down on us at least three or four times. There's no wildlife to be seen, either, when it pours like this," he added.

Eventually we saw stone sheep, mountain goats, bison, moose, elk, caribou, white-tailed and mule deer, wolves, coyotes, foxes, grizzly bears, black bears. And there was one bear in the middle of the road-way—which drank wine from a stemmed glass and almost got us killed, even though it was a figment of my aging imagination.

But even though the bad weather pursued us, I was relieved to have made it into Canada considering the circumstances we had confronted at the border. In retrospect, I admitted that I made a mistake at the border. I told Sam, "I didn't think things out as clearly as I should have, and we were lucky that your mom was available when the border service guy called her—or that she even had her cell phone with her." Patricia tended to lose her keys and forget to charge her cell phone.

But I hadn't actually thought through the entire trip as clearly as I should have, either. I had been invited to speak at a writers' conference in Homer at the tip of the Kenai Peninsula—perhaps, with the exception of Denali, Alaska's most majestic and popular landmark. So I said yes—we would come—Sam and me! A lot of our journeys have come about in that way—I have been invited to Paris, Sydney, Dublin, and Madrid, and I usually accept such invitations because they offer the opportunity to truck with Sam—to share an adventure. In Madrid, we saw The Dyl in concert at a small isolated suburban soccer stadium with no more than a thousand seats. The crowd was very excited and friendly. The fact that we were squeezed together, standing, made no difference whatsoever to anyone. People smoked cigarettes, drank beer; somebody near us, a respectable looking middle-aged couple, sucked on some marijuana through a pipe. Another middle-aged man beside us, cared for by his three teenaged daughters (they lit cigarettes for him and rolled their eyes and laughed at him from time to time), was drunk and nearly out of control, singing, dancing and cheering.

There were no video screens in the small stadium; everyone strained to see Dylan. The sound system was quite good, but The Dyl was a blurry black-hat for most of the concert, weaving in and out of my view. Once, I lifted a very short slight girl in her twenties onto my shoulders. She stayed up for about thirty seconds to see the great man and then asked me to put her down. Later, near the end of the concert, she requested another boost and stayed up there for an entire song, singing and swaying in abandon.

Sam was behind me during all of this, watching the scene with his usual noncommittal expression throughout most of the concert, as if he was too cool to spend much of his time showing the world that he was enjoying himself. I remember being uncomfortable displaying emotions—or even admitting my enjoyment—when I was a teenager having experiences with my parents, so I understood what Sam was doing.

Dylan finished with an encore performance of "Like a Rolling Stone," to which the crowd went screeching, screaming crazy, the entire stadium shaking and rumbling and seemingly falling apart at its core, bending below us. At the end of the song, the band took quick bows and left the stage.

From Sam's journal:

An important element of my truckin' experience is music. It is relaxing, while exciting. It makes me think about things too. But I don't like saying what I think about.

Sometimes Dad asks me, "What are you thinking about?"

I usually give him an answer like, "nothing," even if I am thinking about something, because I don't like to give this private information away. Sometimes, I do want to, and I give him a real answer, and sometimes I am, in fact, thinking about nothing.

The music is fun. It is entertaining. And this is important, because, although I do have my magazines, tablet, and father, there is still not much to do in the truck except look out the window.

Sometimes Dad does not want to listen to music, but NPR, and, although NPR is good in the city, while truckin', I prefer music.

So a note to Dad, for your information, when I say "nothing" when you ask me what I am thinking, it could mean anything. Let's leave it at that.

Anticipation

WHILE WAITING IN LINE for coffee at a rest stop, I watch absent-mindedly through the large front window as Sam wanders out the main entrance to the parking area. Sam is carrying the Coke he has just purchased at an adjoining counter, and he's not paying attention to where he is going as he wanders around, which is why he trips over a high curb and falls flat, sprawling on the sidewalk.

There's hardly anything worse than watching your child suddenly become vulnerable and frightened, thrust into harm's way. You stop whatever you are doing. You freeze. And all of the terrible things, the nightmares and the unmentionables that could happen, go through your mind during that bare naked instant of waiting.

Watching college football on TV, I have always been both annoyed and intrigued by the cameras going back to the mothers of the players and recording each gesture and grimace after every big hit. I can't imagine the torture of seeing your son torpedoed by a human being the size of a Sherman tank, play after play, Saturday after Saturday.

I guess parents can get used to the threat of trauma in the heat of the action; perhaps they get caught up in the game and steel themselves to the possible danger; or only pretend to watch the game—sit in the stands and look at the players moving up and down the field, but not really focusing; it's a blur, a slow-motion haze. Or they don't attend games, don't watch on TV or listen to the radio, and spend their time instead in the garden or with a good book, trying to not think about what might be happening to their precious baby turned into big boy football player until they hear the final score, all the while soothed by the awareness that the phone hasn't been ringing and no one is pounding on the front door with potential bad news.

While mothers' reactions to the big hits are captured frozen in the camera's eye, fathers tend to be isolated on only at the triumphant, victorious moments, like the touchdowns and spectacular catches, as if, somehow, the father has been responsible for the training, the hard work, and the genes that led to his son's athletic prowess and therefore deserves to share the glory of the triumph. It's likely that fathers are bypassed at the traumatic moments because they sublimate the fear and trepidation with a mask of ambivalence, unappealing on camera. Or, after a bit hit, they will laugh, showing bravado, like boxers laughing off their opponents' biggest punches. It's all in the attitude. The dynamics for men and their boys are complicated.

As I watch Sam through the plate glass window trip and belly-flop to the ground and I realize that he is safe from injury, I continue to stand in line, motionless. I want to see if he can recover on his own, and what shape he'll be in when he gets to his feet.

When we started running three years ago, first on the track at Carnegie Mellon University and then subsequently on the Boardwalk in Atlantic City, New Jersey, Sam couldn't or wouldn't maintain a steady running pace. He would run a few steps, then walk, then run again. This was awkward and even more exhausting than the steady, slow, pace I was trying to get him to establish. "Run," I would say. "Bend your knees. Stop walking. Kick it up."

"I know, and I'm trying. Stop nagging."

"It's my job to nag. I'm your father."

I meant this, as Sam very well knew. In our little family, I am the childcare person, the every day, make-sure-Sam-is-ready-for-everything person, while his mom enters into our lives for the big hits—the weekends at the amusement park or wave pool, the late night movie marathons, etc. His mom, a nurse, is highly attuned to science, one of Sam's primary interests; their discussions of anatomy and physiology are intricate and impressive.

But I can't escape the fact that his mom is a woman and I am a man, and there is a significant amount of bonding that only I, a man, can do with Sam. If Sam were a girl, his mother would and should be making similar pronouncements. Women have their own language, rituals, and traditions that are basically baffling to the opposite sex. Sam and I are frequently engaged in horseplay, tickling, poking, pushing, punching, for example, antics women don't quite understand. "Stop it. You guys are crazy; you'll hurt each other; you'll break the furniture," my ex-wife or my mother will yell when we suddenly start to jump up and down on the sofa, pounding each other like madmen. Women have their own brand of bonding, though, secret conversations that leave them laughing and beaming at one another like loons—or, conversely, crying—when men walk into the room.

Sam's mother is probably stricter, much more of a disciplinarian, than I am with Sam. And he listens and responds to her without as much resistance and debate as with me, whose will, it seems, he is always testing—a step beyond horseplay, the beginning of an ongoing battle of wills. But bonding, which is what I am talking about here, is different from discipline.

Sam eventually established a steady jogging pace, although he had tendency to drag his feet. The boards that make up the Boardwalk have weathered indiscriminately and have been replaced haphazardly. Nails are loose and stick up out of the boards. Not lifting his feet was an accident waiting to happen—and it did happen every so often, Sam tripped and, invariably, fell. The dry, splintering wood ripped into his hands and knees, unmercifully.

Sam's responses to tripping and falling come in a rapid succession. First, the injury check in which he is frozen to the ground where he falls, while determining whether he has hurt himself in any serious manner. All of the worst-case scenarios run through your mind—from broken bones, to concussions, to paralysis—and worse—until he and you realize that he will live and that nothing horrible has happened. The next phase is assessing the real damage, mainly cuts, scrapes, and torn clothes. Sometimes you can't do this until you get up and start moving around and this is the phase I am waiting through now at the coffee counter line. What will Sam do? I know what I have taught him to do—to look calm, unperturbed.

Men can't or should not permit themselves to "pose" in weak and vulnerable positions and situations, which is Sam's tendency after falling: freezing, as if the whole world has stopped because he has stopped. Of course for any child in those circumstances, his whole world *has* stopped and there are no other worlds other than the one in which he is the center and nucleus. But jumping up and moving, removing yourself from the limelight, is the manly thing to do. This is basic animal instinct; animals first escape the scene of battle or injury, then whimper and lick their wounds in private. This is exceedingly important for a boy—especiallly one on the cusp of manhood—to learn. The question to ask: When is it time for a father to teach a son when not to show emotion?

Not when it counts, at school when a bunch of thugs are bullying you, for instance, or as an adult in a business situation, when haggling over price for a new warehouse or a bank of computers. On-the-job training for life lessons is something to avoid, if possible.

To save your son heartache, embarrassment and defeat, you teach the rules and explain the complications and ramifications when it doesn't count so much. When there's leeway to lose. Like running on the Boardwalk or tripping on a curb in a parking lot. Not that a father can totally prepare a son for the world awaiting him, but I can give Sam a vital edge. So when Sam trips and falls on the Boardwalk, and the instantaneous agony of phase one passes and I know that nothing serious has happened, my next reaction is to wait, just a split second, to see if he will do the right thing on his own and, if not, to make certain that I trigger it.

"Get up," I say, quietly. Sometimes I will lean forward and whisper in his ear: "Stand up. Keep running. You're ok."

But my subtlety and gentleness can often backfire because Sam is well aware that I have told him repeatedly to pick his feet up and that it is no one's fault but his own that he has fallen, and he is annoyed with himself and about to be annoyed with me because he knows that I am going to tell him sooner or later, "I told you so." And down deep, as annoyed as he will be, Sam wants me to remind him of his mistake because he knows—it is unspoken—that he has to learn these lessons, no matter how difficult and painful, and that I am doing my job as a father, the same job he will have to do perhaps twenty years from now when he ventures into fatherhood. And of course Sam knows, also, that people are watching and that the pressure is on him to pass a test that has been inadvertently thrust upon him, when, as a child, he hasn't asked for it, doesn't want it or deserve it. It's all part of the mysterious and completely ridiculous adult world, which he is inheriting and forced to tolerate.

At the rest stop, I watch as Sam stands, picks up his paper cup of Coke, half empty, and limps off to the side, away from the bystanders watching him, in order to compose himself. Later, after I get my coffee and we meet back at the truck, he doesn't mention his accident and neither do I. His knee is skinned and slightly bleeding, tears are welling in his eyes, but we don't say a word about it.

Sam's Journal—from 2003:

These past days, I did two things that I am amazed I actually had the courage to just say I would go and do.

First of all, I ran twelve miles. This was from the Ventnor end of the Boardwalk, six miles to the Atlantic City end, and back. I think the primary reason I was able to do this was the good, breezy, mild, cool weather. The next day, my dad and I rode back to Pittsburgh in our truck . I soon met up with my mom and we went to Kennywood, a world-famous amusement park in Pittsburgh, and rode the Phantom's Revenge, a world-famous ride. It takes you up seventy-five feet, about forty-five seconds, and drops sharply down on a curve again, and then goes up another hill on the momentum, down to the ground, down a hill, almost straight down. Then it shakes you up like crazy. I had done this ride before—and run eleven miles, almost twelve, before, but since I hadn't done either for a while, I got concerned about both, even though it wasn't reasonable (and I knew it).

I wouldn't say I was afraid—I knew both the run and the ride would be fine. But then, once I planned the run—and locked myself into a promise and a plan of both my dad and myself—once I got on that ride—and physically locked myself in a car—the anticipation got tough. In the few days before the run, in the forty-five seconds before the drop, I tried not to think about it, but it kept nagging at me, basically asking the question: "How torturous will it be?" and I knew neither would be terrible, although it could be a bit tough. And once it's done, the anticipation is gone; you relax again, as if you would have canceled it. And after the ride, I did it twice again. Most of all, after the run (my longest ever), I said I could do two more miles. I learned something important—the run proposed it, the ride proved it: it's the anticipation that hurts, not the task.

Tuna Fish Trouble

ALTHOUGH WE WERE two guys on the road sharing books, music and ideas, it goes without saying that we didn't always get along. I suspect Hopper and Fonda didn't see eye-to-eye, everyday, all the time, nor Dean and Sal either. Girls, booze, and drugs could fracture the best of friendships; but for Sam and me, one day, on the road, the worst disagreement we ever had was caused by tuna fish salad sandwiches. This happened when we were on the way to the Grand Canyon.

It all began when Sam, while surfing on his computer the night before, discovered that one of his favorite movies—*X-Men*—was going to be playing on one of the cable networks that evening. He said he wanted to stop early enough in our travels to watch it. I didn't like this idea, and I told him so. Here we are in an incredible journey of exploration and discovery, and you want to delay it? You choose *X-Men* to the adventure of the open road?

I should have never asked. Of course, he would choose watching *X-Men* in his bed in a hotel room over riding in the cab of a pick-up truck with his old fart of a father. Wouldn't any kid? But I was too dense to acknowledge that reality, so I argued, and he argued back.

We went back and forth. I was indignant; he was persistent. The rhetoric escalated. We said things neither of us meant—stupid things—

You're shallow; all you care about are movies and games. There's more to life—

You're selfish; all you care about is yourself and your writers' conference speeches—

Your character is flawed—
I'm going home on the next bus—
I dare you—
I'm outta here—
If you leave, I will never talk to you again; our relationship will be over,
forever—
That's fine with me; I'm going home—
You're inconsiderate—
You're not my dad—
I no longer have a son—

It went on and on. But then when Sam began screaming at me and the entire situation had escalated way out of control, I uttered the words I had been holding back from the beginning of our conversation, waiting for the opening, the opportune moment to say them: "Tuna fish salad sandwich," I said triumphantly. "Tuna fish salad sandwich," I repeated. My timing was impeccable. No other four words in the English language could have been more effective and, in retrospect, more inappropriate in that situation than "tuna fish salad sandwich."

WHEN IT COMES to food, Sam has an enduring penchant for blandness. Traveling, however, you realize the extent to which people will go out of their way to elaborate on the pure perfection of the plainest foods. Few restaurants begin with the basics anymore. Every eating establishment, from chic cafés to barebones diners, needs to demonstrate creative energy—or justify outrageous prices by the extent and range of the adornments they provide with their menu items. Pancakes and waffles with powdered sugar, assorted fruits, whipped cream, flavored butters, right on your plate whether you want it or not. With grilled cheese are cups of coleslaw, honeydew slices, green onions, carrot sticks, or tomatoes. Pickle chips are the worst because the brine dribbles down the plate and soaks the toast.

For Sam, and others sharing an obsession for the bare basics, the grilled cheese bread must be white and not one of those health breads with nuts, sunflower seeds, or dried fruits. The cheese should be American—not cheddar, Monterey Jack, or—certainly not, for God's sake—provolone. Which is another serious breech of decorum and tradition. Why won't restaurants in America sell the cheese named for the country? This is the patriotic thing to do, like pins of the American flag on politician's lapels. American cheese for America is a no-brainer. Once in Canada, a waitress thought she could find plain white bread in the kitchen for Sam, but American cheese left her clueless "It's the cheese with chemicals," Sam said.

"Oh, yes," she replied. "I've heard of that."

AFTER MY TUNA FISH salad sandwich declaration, the silence in the truck was deafening and the tension thick as butter. We had started the morning listening, as always, to the Truckin' song, the third track on the "Best of The Grateful Dead" album. After "Truckin'," Sam will always ask me which of the Rolling Stones albums I want to hear first, but this time he made the choice on his own. Most disputes between Sam and me are related to food because, often, I can't get him what he wants to eat. So I try to order food that I think he is going to like, as close as possible to his parameters, but not the same things, and I frequently fail, and I am stuck paying a check for uneaten food with the burden of an even hungrier child. And then, sometimes, after I find him the kind of plain food he wants and I am feeling triumphant, he doesn't eat it right away. Sam will contemplate white pizza or a grilled American cheese for fifteen minutes, staring at the food while chewing thoughtfully on piece and after piece of bread with butter. Or staring at nothing at all—into space and time—for hours, sometimes, before eating. He wants the food in front of him.

Watching Sam not eat after I have worked so hard to find food that passes the Sam blandness challenge becomes a silent test of wills. Who blinks first? Me, by demanding and then begging that he eat? Or Sam, who is staring at the food, finally taking a bite and giving it the taste test? "Why don't you just make him eat what you put on his plate—or let him go hungry?" people ask repeatedly. "He won't starve," they tell me, as if I don't already know this. I understand and respect their questions and advice. Tough love can work. But unless a child is grossly underweight or obese or his pediatrician determines he is not ingesting enough fiber or whatever, what's the point of playing policeman?

Why do I want my son to be unhappy or to be hungry when, if I put in a little extra effort and money, I can please him and get him what he wants most of the time? For sure, it causes ongoing problems; I get frustrated chasing around for restaurants and convenience stores with Sam-friendly food, and the chase causes tension between us. But I am willing to grit my teeth and, as I always tell him, "service his account," because, for one thing, I have the time and energy to do it, and for another thing, I think maybe Sam has gotten cheated by ending up with an old-fart dad; there will be a time, perhaps, when I can't do very much for him, and he might have to be servicing my account, God forbid. He might be feeding me!

So let's just say I am paying him off in advance, although, as I say, sometimes I get so annoyed I get carried away, complaining and criticizing and threatening, that I turn myself into a Nazi dad. I hate that, but it happens. There are triggers that make it happen, like this tuna fish salad sandwich business. I was sorry I brought it up—it was a mistake, but I was stuck—we were stuck together—with it.

Sam did not speak for a long time after I said, "tuna fish salad sandwich." And then, after at least a dozen Rolling Stones tracks, he replied to my "tuna fish salad sandwich" attack with his own very few words—words he would remain adamant about until hell froze over—or at least until I froze over. Sam said those words softly, looking straight ahead out the window, just as The Mick was wailing "You Can't Always Get What You Want."

"No way tuna fish," Sam said, "Not ever."

The moment that Sam uttered those words in such an adamant and unyielding way, I realized that I had to take some action. If there would be any backing down, it would have to come from me—the dad—and not the son.

Sam's Journal:

I found out that one of my favorite movies, X-Men, was going to be on the FX channel at eight o'clock that night, and I told Dad that I wanted to see it so we should stop truckin' early. But Dad said he needed or wanted to get somewhere, and so we would truck on longer than usual, maybe; we could always buy X-Men on pay-per-view at almost any hotel, if we missed it.

But the highway was crowded, for some reason, and it was one of those nights—we have had plenty of them—when all the hotels were filled up. Dad took us on an annoying roundabout maze to find a place to stay. At one point, and I can't remember why anymore, I urged him to turn left. I said it over and over. Left, left, left. Left was the way to go to find a hotel, I just knew it. But Dad wouldn't, and then I insisted. Pretty soon Dad started to shout and point at me, and guess what he was saying, over and over, as he shouted? "TUNA FISH SANDWICH! TUNA FISH SANDWICH."

So now Dad was going to force me to pay off my bet because I had lost my temper and eat the tuna fish sandwich. Well, I told him, I wouldn't eat it. No way, Jose, as my mother says.

He went on and on ("TUNA FISH SALAD SANDWICH! TUNA FISH SALAD SANDWICH.") But I didn't say a word. I wasn't going to do what I wasn't going to do.

Sam's Dangerous Disease

"DON'T PUT THE CAMERA on me; I don't want to see myself all the time," I had told Sam at breakfast the previous morning. If I told him once, I told him a thousand times.

"But you're the interviewer. I'm watching you."

"I know I will be asking the questions, but viewers will be interested in the people answering—not asking. Let the faces and places of America fill your viewfinder!" This was a bold and dramatic statement, a call to action he could hardly forget. Yet, how did I not realize that Sam's independent nature, combined with his chronic disease I call "DontListenToDadUntilHeLoseshisTemper-itis" would hold sway?

This is how the whole tuna fish salad trouble had started—with something stupid and totally unimportant—the video camera, for God's sake. I couldn't get Sam to focus on the cinematic task and understand—or care—about framing his shots and footage. In retrospect, I can see, understand, that video means nothing, in the scheme of things. Nice for others, but for Sam and me, we don't need video; we have our experiences, our memories, our feelings. But I wasn't so logical and patient, bristling with such maturity and wisdom, then.

Practicing with the camera the weeks before our journey, Sam had focused all creative energies on my nose, with special attention on the depth and circumference of my nostrils. It never occurred to me that my nose was any larger or more inelegantly shaped than most anyone else's, but Sam's blatant use of probing close-ups, backlighting and the other special effects offered in digital abundance by the Sony Corporation made me look grotesque, like a villainous character in a James

Bond movie—or a waiter at The Carnegie Deli. After much yelling and screaming, followed by begging, pleading, and reasoning, and concluding with a threat to confiscate the camera, all of his computers and to crush his skull with a cement block, Sam's "Dont-Listen-To-Dad-Until-He-Loses-His-Temper-itis" seemed to subside and my nose and nostrils lost their fascination—until we headed west.

I explained to Sam how important it was to capture conversations of other people as we traveled—both tourists and people indigenous to where we were visiting. And get a lot of road shots—so that viewers can see the country changing in shape, the color of the landscape, the big blue sky. By "viewers," I meant friends and family; I didn't really think we had an HBO special going, but I figured that getting the entire experience on video would be a perfect way to remember what and who we saw; the book we are writing—this book—was obviously my idea, and Sam, generously and faithfully went along with it.

I also figured Sam to be the preferred cameraperson because few folks could object when a kid recorded their every movement—and even the intimacies of their noses. And he was too shy to engage with the person being recorded on his own. But as a videographer, Sam was a total washout. If only Sam and I could have performed a person-merge, with the Sam part taking control of all the technical aspects of the Sony, all the buttons and switches and concepts that eluded me, while the me part performed the interview and recorded it at the same time.

As WE SAT AT breakfast the morning the tuna fish salad sandwich trouble had started, previewing the rushes of the previous few days, I discovered that the camera—or Sam—had dogged me in every direction. There were scenes of me walking, talking, scratching, eating, and driving. The walking scenes highlighted my butt and how big it is; the talking scenes featured close-ups of my mouth and tongue; Sam seemed to know instinctively when I would be scratching my privates and would focus the camera in the exact correct position to record it, as well as while I was eating, with ketchup, ice cream, mayonnaise, and other disgusting junk on my lips, nose, and beard. For variety, Sam also collected close-ups of the dashboard of the truck, with periodic glimpses of my hands on the steering wheel, with dramatic frozen-frame shots of my cuticles in sepia tones.

To be fair, there are other people in Sam's videos—or parts of other people, like a waiter's finger as he writes down our order, or a pedestrian's body parts—rear-end, ankle, earlobe, separated, hanging in limbo as they walk down the street. When there is more than one person in the scene, Sam usually endeavors, utilizing the Sony technology available to him on the mini-cam, to get pieces of all of them (three half heads, for example, of three different people in various sepia shades, connected randomly to each other like human Tinker Toys) and there's no sound whatsoever from these subjects, except background noise, because Sam is standing too far away to record what they are saying. So, even when I interview these folks, you can't hear my question or their answers.

Sitting at breakfast, I became so annoyed watching these rushes, realizing (or fantasizing) that I had had some pretty terrific conversations that were totally lost—audio and visual—that I said, slamming my fist down on the table and raising my voice, "Damn it, Sam, this is some of the worst video I have ever seen!" I understood immediately, the moment that my temper flared, that getting upset with my son over a video, even though he has portrayed me as a walrus in Levi's and T-shirt, is completely inappropriate, a realization that seemed not to affect my indignation, for I went on and on, criticizing and complaining, thoughtlessly.

This is so frustrating—and it happens more often than I like to admit. I hear myself whining about something with Sam, and I am personally embarrassed by what I sound like as I listen to myself, and I know I should shut up and put the problem or complaint behind me, which would be the mature thing to do, and I have all intention to do so, immediately. But then, God knows why, I don't. *I just don't.* I continue to whine, and I know—I can hear myself—I sound like such a fool, like a parent of whom I would be harshly critical were I to overhear this ridiculous nonsense, overbearing, unacceptable. But I can't seem to stop.

Sam is much more mature and controlled than me. After eating his pancakes and bacon, watching the rushes with me, and then listening to me complain, on and on, Sam calmly admitted: "The video sucks. But now," he added, looking up from his pancakes and directly into my eyes, pausing to take advantage of this dramatic moment, "you owe me."

And I realized, alas—and I was far past embarrassment and deeply into the mortification zone—that my son was absolutely right. I owed him big-time. I reached into my pocket, came up with a mound of crushed currency—I tend to ball-up my bills and shove them into my pockets; I never know how much cash I have—and dug out two five-dollar bills. In the truck, yesterday, Sam and I had discussed the fact that although we were having great fun, that the day sometimes gets wearing and we lose our tempers in such close quarters over small matters, mostly, and we say things to one another we don't really mean. So I had proposed that every time I lost my temper from that point onward, I would pay him ten dollars if, every time he went off the deep end and got angry, he would try to eat something he had never before tried. So this time I lost my money—fast.

But then today in the truck he had lost his temper over not being able to see *X-Men*, and for a minute I thought I would be able to win back my money—and a bit of my pride—by demanding he eat a tuna fish salad sandwich—but Sam wasn't buying it. He wouldn't give in. On the one hand, I was right—totally right. Sam and I had made a bet. I lost my temper first and paid up—ten dollars. Then he had lost his temper, and he should be mature enough to pay as well and keep his word—eating a tuna fish salad sandwich. As we rocketed up the road, listening to our music and staring straight ahead, pretending that the other person in the cab didn't exist, I tried to decide what to do next.

My father used to say that a man is not a man if he doesn't keep his word. A man's word is his bond—his badge of honor. No matter how rich and powerful and famous you are, my dad would say, when you come right down to it, a person is worth no more than the pledges and promises he has made and honored. I didn't agree with most of my father's ideas, but I will acknowledge the importance of that particular point of view—and I believe in it, as a principle, wholeheartedly. You don't make promises you don't intend to keep, and I have said that to Sam, repeatedly. Sam should definitely try to eat the tuna fish salad sandwich. That is the right thing to do. "Try the tuna fish salad," I said to him. "Take a bite." But he doesn't want to—he will not even answer me. So now it has become a big issue—escalating well beyond the meaning of the incident and each of our best intentions—so what is a father to do? How rigid should a father be?

I think of the movie *The Great Santini* (from the Pat Conroy novel), for which Robert Duvall received an Academy Award nomination. Duvall plays Wilbur "Bull" Meechum, a cocky, arrogant Marine Corps fighter pilot who is impatient with his life in the military during peacetime and takes his frustration out on his family. He hammers and baits his eldest son, Ben, a teenager, relentlessly until, in a one-on-one backyard basketball game, his son fights back, and the family cheers Ben's efforts.

Meechum actually loses the one-on-one and can't accept the obvious, that Ben has turned a corner and found his own confidence and voice. Humiliated, Meechum continues to hover around the backboard, dribbling, shooting, practicing through the entire night—sharpening his game for a rematch the following morning. It is a pitiful, searing scene.

The circumstances surrounding our tuna fish sandwich controversy are a little different, I know. I am not drinking (Meechum was an alcoholic) and I am not trying to bully Sam, but I am trying to teach him a lesson and get him to do something he doesn't really want to do, even though he promised. Although he is young, Sam has always known how to fight back, not with his fists, but his own iron will.

A few years ago, Sam and I were riding bikes together. There was one long hill to conquer in our bike route up Beechwood Blvd. Sometimes Sam would stop and walk when the hill became too much for him. But I had discovered that by offering him extra time at the computer I could inspire him to pedal to the top. I continued to add to the route and the hill by building in a series of side trips in order to keep up the pressure and challenge him—until one day I realized I had taken the challenge too far—and he snapped.

No more than ten yards into that final hill, Sam stopped peddling and dropped his bike to the ground. "I am not going any further," he said simply. "I quit." I pushed his bike to the top of the hill and eventually convinced him to ride home downhill, but I knew by the look on his face and the tension between us that the comfort and camaraderie that had previously existed when we biked together might not be duplicated in the near future. I was right. Sam had his limits, and I was proud of him for that.

And I had learned a lesson. There's a balance between what you think you need to teach your son and the influence and guidance your son, as he grows older, is willing to accept. I try to remember that my son is learning from me everyday, whether I realize it or not—the good and the bad—and that what I do, how I conduct myself, will indirectly shape his character.

Bull Meechum didn't realize that he was the role model his son had most access to and that he, Bull, as a young man, would have never tolerated from his own father the rigidity he was displaying toward his own son. Ben responded to Bull like Bull would have responded in the same situation, sooner or later. Today in the truck, Sam was, in fact, following my lead by doing what I had taught him—to not become someone else's person and to follow his own heart and conscience. No doubt it was wrong to refuse to pay the tuna fish salad sandwich debt and I am hoping that I can get him to understand his mistake, but I will not attempt to bludgeon my son into doing something to which he is opposed. And if keeping your word is a lesson to teach a son—and it is—than another lesson has to do with compromise, and with learning how to move forward in life in a way that brings people together rather than consistently dividing them.

"Sam," I say, after a while, "do you remember when we went to the Rock and Roll Museum in Cleveland?

Yes," he said. His voice was stiff, but not cold and resistant.

"Do you remember The Mick film clip?" The Mick is walking through a crowd of fans and paparazzi. He is dressed in the flamboyant, outrageous hippie style for which he and so many other rock stars of that generation were known—tie-died shirt, silk jacket with bold pastel stripes, super-tight trousers, pointed-toe black boots—and, Keith Richards, weighed down by a yoke of bejeweled necklaces and grotesque finger rings, walking right behind The Mick, says something. His mouth moves, though we can't make out what he is saying, but The Mick turns, suddenly, angrily, and pushes and then threatens, seemingly, to punch Richards.

"Remember," I reminded him. "You said. 'I thought they were friends.' You were surprised how they behaved toward one another."

He nodded.

"They were—and they *are* friends," I said. "But they had some bad moments together at the height of their fame—and had a temporary falling out." I know that "the height of their fame" sounds kind of silly because the Stones seem to be forever achieving new heights of fame. Sam nodded. I am not certain he is following me, exactly. I try something else.

"Simon and Garfunkel? You know the guys from the 'Bookends' album we like so much? They made such sweet music together—and then they didn't talk with one another for twenty-five years."

Again, he looked at me expectantly. "Do you know what I'm saying, Sam? I don't want to do that with you. I don't want to waste twenty-five minutes let alone twenty-five years not being together with you, on the same wavelength. I'm sorry if I made you angry," I said. "The tuna fish salad sandwich had nothing to do with *X-Men*. I realize that now."

I am not certain what exactly went through Sam's mind at that moment, but I do know that he was relieved that I had broken the ice. I could hear the strain dissipate from his voice, as I knew he could hear the tension and anxiety I had been feeling drain from mine. "I'm sorry that I tried to force the tuna fish sandwich on you. I shouldn't have done it. But I also think you should have kept your promise and tried a bite of tuna salad—it wouldn't have killed you—and you made a bet. A bet is a bet. So let us say we both made errors and leave it at that."

It was over then—beautifully. A cascade of emotional regrets poured from both of us, almost simultaneously.

You're right Dad. I lost my temper, and I shouldn't have.

We both said bad things to one another.
I meant them when I said them, but I don't mean them anymore.
But once you say things they're out in the open. You're declaring yourself.
No matter if you do not mean them anymore, they're still real. Words never go away. You need to always remember that fact.
I know, it wasn't right. I'm sorry. I apologize. Words are real.
Words are everything, almost—
But, he added after a while, *I still don't want to eat a tuna fish sandwich.*

I looked at him carefully and he looked back at me, his eyes not wavering against my intense glare. I decided to drop the point and let it pass. I had gone as far as he would let me. A father needs to know when to stop.

"Let's blame it on the doodah man," I said, referring to the doodah man in the truckin' song lyrics (*Truckin.' Got my chips cashed in. Keep Truckin.' Like the doodah Man*), who's kind of a mystery figure, although we assumed, without much evidence, that he was the Grateful Dead's pusher—their source for drugs. The doodah man upset our karma and somehow created a sense of negativity between us. He was the evil truckin' monster. We would treat each other with overwhelming consideration from now on, thereby destroying the doodah man, forever. The doodah man is toast, we said. That was that.

Sam's Journal:

We drove on for a long time in silence. Dad and I were both pissed. We finally found a hotel room. It was very late by then, long past X-Men. It was at a not-so-nice hotel. The whole building was literally one room, except for the guest rooms, utility rooms and bathrooms. This included the pool. Strategically located in the center of the main room, its location ensured that there was humidity enough to allow tropical rainforest animals as guests, and when someone with a room on an interior balcony corridor leaves their room, the first thing they would see is ... you in the pool, half naked. We didn't like this place.

We ate pizza. At some point, Dad said I didn't ever have to eat tuna fish even though I lost my bet, technically. He apologized for losing his temper and he canceled the ten-dollar deal from that moment on for both of us.

Another Border Crossing

WE BRACED OURSELVES for the inevitable interrogation—and the doom of exile—when we neared the border connecting British Columbia and Alaska. The border guard had warned us back at Portal about the mean, rotten U.S. border guards, ("Worse than us, I assure you!"), and we were taking his warnings quite seriously. But this time we were better prepared. I had my story straight and we knew what to expect.

I had the letter Patricia had faxed attesting to my good character, the legitimacy of my fatherhood, and her total willingness to release her child to me. The guardhouse at the border was very similar to the one at the Portal-Canada line, and I said to Sam, "Look for the signs, Sam. We might have to wait. I don't want to miss anything telling me to wait. We're starting off without proper documentation in the first place, so let's at least behave appropriately."

I slowed to a stop, ready, bracing myself for whatever happened next. I look my driver's license out of my wallet. But then, just like at Portal, no one came immediately to deal with us.

We sat in the truck. "So we are waiting," I said. "Except this time, we know what we are doing. We are waiting."

"We'll wait and wait," said Sam.

"We'll wait forever, if that's what it takes," I said with resolve. "Now we know what they want—they want us to wait and so we'll wait."

Which is when the border patrol officer poked his head out of the guardhouse window and asked for our passports. We explained what had happened at Portal and the mistake I made for not bringing proper I.D. for Sam.

The guard listened as I talked and shook his head, smiling, although you could tell he was amused only by my stupidity.

"Can we go?" I asked after telling him the story and showing him Patricia's fax.

"We can be more lenient here than they will be in the lower forty-eight when you try to get back into the country. So yes, you can go. But you ought to have better I.D. before you make the crossing again." He added simply: "Welcome to the United States," he said.

And that was that—for the moment.

From Sam's Journal:

One time I got us lost, and my dad was angry with me, and he wouldn't stop complaining, even after we got back on track. Then, right after we crossed from Canada back into the United States, we saw a landmark. STARBUCKS. Dad got a cup of Starbucks and me a chocolate chip cookie, because I often look for junk food on the road, which is why my mom wants me to eat an apple a day. Dad was happy and no longer angry. He loves Starbucks. The end.

Buttering Toast

NO MATTER HOW OLD I get and how much I experience and accomplish, who I am and what I am as a father and a man seem sometimes so elusive. Some of this insecurity and divisiveness has to do with the phases and definitions of age:

First I am young, then I am middle aged, and finally, shamefully, I am old, although in my head I remain young, the same person I was in high school or in the military or, a few years later, the anxious and enthusiastic young man trying to achieve success in my writing career. All of these years happen in a flash—seemingly simultaneously, squashed together. They are over and done with, it seems, before I understand that they have even started.

Doggedly, I try to establish a foundation and a rationale for my personality and behavior as a model for Sam, but even after being alive for so many years, I sometimes feel confused and unfocused. Which is why perhaps my signals to Sam are sometimes off the mark. In retrospect, I think that my shameful behavior in relation to toast buttering was rooted in the scope of Alaskan culture and the rugged pioneering spirit that is so vital there, although that is a rationale and not an excuse. I am just thinking that I might not have made an issue out of it, if we had been somewhere in the lower 48. On second thought, I take that back: toast buttering was on my mind long before Alaska.

The one thing I can say in my favor in response to my behavior is that I am so conscientious and so afraid of doing the wrong thing in relation to my son that I constantly monitor myself, continually replaying in my mind the scenarios we share, so that my frequent mistakes can be rectified—repeatedly.

IN THE HOTEL restaurant during the writers' conference, Sam is buttering his toast at breakfast. He dabs the toast with his butter knife as if he is finger-painting, spreading little portions of butter over small areas of the bread. This process gets on my nerves rather quickly. It has been going on for a long time; he puts butter on his pancakes or waffles in the same way—*dab-dab-dab* after dainty dab. He addresses his burgers and hotdogs in a similar fashion, adding ketchup gingerly, dabbing rather than shaking or spreading, the manly thing to do.

At first, I thought that Sam would grow out of this awkward, effeminate toast-buttering tendency. I blamed it on his youth and lack of coordination and figured that by the time he turned thirteen he'd have more manly mannerisms. Thirteen was arbitrary, but I sometimes cling to the bar mitzvah age line. Bar mitzvah means manhood. This was a big joke, even when I turned thirteen a million years or so ago.

My father took away all of my bar mitzvah money—the gifts I had received—because he didn't think I was responsible enough to manage all that cash—nearly five hundred dollars, which was big bucks back then. I think he thought I would spend it all in Steubenville, Ohio. He would have been mistaken—at least in the short run.

I was a virgin at the time of my bar mitzvah and would remain so for three more years until I was old enough to drive (sixteen) to my first (but not my last!) whorehouse. The best whorehouses were in Steubenville, although my buddies and I would also drive to Wheeling, West Virginia, across the Ohio River from Steubenville, where more whorehouses existed. We wanted variety—and discount prices. Two dollars was a lot to spend for five minutes (or less) of sex. And we wanted to sample the differences between West Virginia women and Ohio women. We theorized that the whores in Ohio would be cleaner and more highly educated than those in West Virginia—this was obvious to us, although, as it turned out, ill conceived, since the same whores in Steubenville one week would show up in Wheeling the following week. We were also looking for Jewish prostitutes. Most of the whores we asked about religion were noncommittal, although a couple I talked with offered to consider converting to Judaism for an extra two dollars.

I am, by the way, not faulting my father for not letting me spend my bar mitzvah money. It was probably the practical thing to do, since I might have been able to get to Steubenville sooner had I had this money in my sweaty horny palms when I was thirteen, although at the time of my bar mitzvah, I knew very little of what sex was all about—or even horniness—which I assumed then was the feeling I got in response to loneliness and isolation rather than physical longing. Life is one long, hard trek to Joy City, which is often, you eventually discover, not the paradise you thought it would be.

Sam did not become a bar mitzvah boy; he is the youngest avowed atheist I have ever met. But he knows a lot more about sex than I did at his age, due to his sex education classes in school, the R-rated movies I take him to, and the online sites I suspect he visits in secret. He turned thirteen in January—about six months before we took off on this AlCan odyssey—and I have been on edge ever since, anticipating change in his personality and in my relationship with him. I wrote this in my journal, on his thirteenth birthday:

"I fear that a reversal will be occurring in my life with Sam, a radical shift, now that he is thirteen. Perhaps it is already in process now that he has had his birthday. Everything in my life is changing in front of my eyes. By the end of the summer, Sam will no longer be the Sam I know, and all of the people in my life will be different, except, I fear, for me. I will be the same, in the middle of this cauldron of change, decimated by the loss, floundering to adjust. Sinking, perhaps?"

So far, nothing like this has happened, thank goodness. My son may have matured when he turned thirteen, but he's pretty much the same kid he was at twelve. But he still doesn't know about macho toast buttering—which was something I was trying to teach him, part of my fatherly responsibilities. I had a lot to learn, macho-wise, myself, however.

As I WATCH SAM buttering his toast, I try not to say anything, to let things happen and let Sam deal with his toast on his own. I nag Sam so often about everything under the sun, so I figure he can butter his toast any way he wants, whether I like it or not. At least, that is what I repeat to myself again and again, as I sit there, watching him dab and dab. But I quickly run out of patience and good intentions. "Sam, why do you have to butter your toast like you're gay?" I suddenly blurt out.

"What do you mean?" he asks. Sam has a pretty good sense of humor, although I cannot always distinguish between a good time to tease him and a bad time—and where the borderline between acceptable and unacceptable teasing falls on any given day. But how do you teach a teenage boy to be manly or masculine? Do you *want* to teach a teenage boy to be manly and masculine, actually, I ask myself? I consider for a while. In Alaska, in the land of these independent rugged individualists, I conclude, I think I do.

But first I try to make a joke out of it by acting out the difference between how a gay person and a macho man would butter toast. I use sweeping, clumsy, boorish gestures to demonstrate the latter. I am petite, dainty, and precise for the former.

Sam laughs—I have made a connection. Fathers sometimes have to be clowns to make a point. Just a few years ago, I would act out the difference between fathers and mothers, men and women, by purring like a kitten or roaring like a lion. When I roared, I puffed up my cheeks and pounded my chest with my fists, and when I purred I made my face look droopy and my voice falsetto. Maybe this is unfair—and sexist. But sometimes you have to be outrageous or politically incorrect to make a point.

Like I keep telling Sam, I want him to act in the way in which he is most comfortable, but I also want him to be aware of his actions and their ramifications. "People will not only hear your words, but they will notice the tone of your voice. They will interpret everything—from the way you butter toast to how you swing your arms when you walk down the street."

"I just like to be careful and thorough," Sam says. "I want the butter evenly divided on the toast. I like it better that way. The taste, I mean. It has nothing to do with anything else."

But then I add a clarifying point. "It doesn't matter to me if you are gay or not," I tell him. "I will always love you."

I don't know why I tell him this, since I don't think he is gay and this isn't the question we are discussing here at the moment, anyway. But then, abruptly, I take it back. I want to clarify further. I am not sure I have been totally forthcoming. "You be what and who you want to be or feel you need to be—whatever makes you happy and allows you to make a contribution to the world in one way or another."

But in retrospect, as I hear those words play back to me, I realize I am lying to Sam, and he and I know it. I need to be more forthcoming; I owe my son that. I try again: "It actually does matter if you are gay," I tell him. "On second thought."

"How do you mean?" he asks.

"Your life will be more complicated. Assholes like me will be noting the fag-like way you butter your toast and conceivably making an issue out of it. Life may be more difficult, not that I think you can do anything about it."

Sam doesn't reply. He's listening carefully, waiting for something to happen, I don't know what—or for me to say more. Sam is smart enough to want complete information—to delve into and discuss important topics. "But it doesn't mean I will love you any less," I add, after a while. "In fact," I continue, rolling my eyes and winking, "it might mean I will love you more."

"Thanks Dad," Sam says, as he puffs his cheeks in a lion-like way, pounds the table with his fist and begins buttering his toast as if he is drunk. Butter and toast crumbs and silverware are flying all over the place.

"Good job, Sam," I tell him. "Now you're acting like a real man."

NOT THAT I CAN pretend to know what being a real man is all about—or how an old man is supposed to feel and act.

At the conclusion of my reading at the writers conference, a twenty-four year-old girl, a college graduate, soon to be entering into a graduate program, comes up and says, "I want to tell you how much I respect you. I admire so much how you conduct yourself. I wish you were my father."

I look at her, absolutely astounded. I am caught totally off-guard. Here is this beautiful fresh-faced blond child, looking up at me adoringly. She's calling me "sensei," she's telling me that all she ever wanted in her life is to spend quality time with her father, travel with her father like I am traveling with my Sam. I know from reading some of her writing that her father has recently died of cancer and that her younger brother is a heroin addict. I know that she's a free spirit, a graduate of the Waldorf School, that she does her own thing, just like her father, who had many different professions, including Baptist preacher and door-to-door life insurance salesman.

I know that yesterday she lost her wallet and was standing on the veranda in front of the hotel, weeping and totally helpless and afraid in response to her loss. All of her identification was missing, which meant, among other things, that the new bartender at the hotel that night would not recognize her and therefore not sell her beer. What a thing to worry about.

I remember thinking then about how world-wise she was on the one hand. She had experienced more sadness in her short life, with her father dead after a painful debilitating illness and her brother systematically destroying himself, than I had experienced in my own very long (in comparison) lifespan. But on the other hand, she was weeping like a baby, wishing for help from her mother, whom she was trying desperately to reach on her cell phone, because of a lost wallet and a missing beer connection.

And now, this beautiful young thing who knows both nothing and everything, is standing there, looking up at me, adoringly—I have remained at my perch on an elevated podium—telling me that she admires what I stand for more than anyone alive on earth and that she wishes that I was her father.

I am listening, feeling flummoxed that she or anyone one else could admire such a fucking faker as me. For, as she is lavishing this blanket of praise on me, and I am sucking in her compliments with quiet modesty, my thoughts are fixed firmly on the plunging neckline of her loose-fitting summer cotton dress and those breasts of hers, bouncing like voluptuous beanbags in front of my eyes.

Don't get me wrong. It is not that I am conceiving of this little girl as a woman I want to try to sleep with. Her fresh, as-yet-unspoiled innocence is appealing. But I am, if nothing else, an eminently practical middle-aged man. I take chances—I can be daring—I have been dangerously daring—but I try to avoid foolish and irrational risks.

No conceivable pleasure can equal the inevitable disappointment of such a gambit, assuming that the scenario I am imagining here is even possible. Do admiring groupies who consider you a father figure also want to sleep with you? I don't think so. But how is it that this fully developed woman can conceive of me as a father figure? Am I that old? Is she contemplating my silver hair and crinkled puffy face in the same manner as I am regarding her beanbag breasts? This is unsettling. Am I a man or a father? In my mind, I am both and I am neither.

THE FAMOUS AUTHOR William Styron once taught me that the prostate makes all men equal.

Styron, author of, among other brilliant books, *The Confessions of Nat Turner* and *Sophie's Choice*, was in Pittsburgh to give a Saturday evening reading at a conference. His agent picked him up at the airport late Friday night and dropped him off at a reception in his honor. The agent's family lived in the city, so she made Styron's appearance a tax-deductible reason to weekend here.

Pittsburgh is overloaded with families of famous people who once lived here and don't anymore. Rob Marshall, Annie Dillard, David McCullough, and Dan Marino are rooted in Pittsburgh. Actor Jeff Goldblum even made a movie about returning to Pittsburgh to visit. The agent, anxious to see her parents, left the party early, but Styron wanted to party a while longer. I volunteered to take him back to his hotel.

Styron died in 2008, but he was a charming southern gentleman with wavy white hair and an unpretentious formality. He drank and chatted with the women, mostly, and we closed the party down. In my car, heading for his hotel, he suddenly remembered that he forgot to retrieve his luggage from his agent's car. Worse, his agent used her married name; he didn't know her family name so we couldn't look it up in the phonebook. The information operator was not helpful, and when we telephoned the agent's home phone in Washington where she lived, thinking that maybe her husband would provide the necessary information, we got an answering machine. This was before everyone had a cell phone.

Now we were riding around in the car, late Friday night turning into early Saturday morning. The roads were empty, the bars and restaurants long past closing, the city dark and dead.

"We'll go to a convenience store, and you can get what you need for the night—an extra toothbrush, stuff like that," I said.

"It's not brushing my teeth I am worrying about," Styron told me. "I need to pee. In fact," he hesitated. "I will need to pee soon." Then he added, for emphasis: "Very soon." His prostate medicine was in that suitcase.

So there I was, sitting in my car in the dark in the middle of my hometown with William Styron, the great Pulitzer-prize winning author and a close friend of Hillary and Bill Clinton, Jesse Jackson, and God knows who else. For months, I had looked forward to this weekend so that I could momentarily rub elbows with Styron and perhaps in some way gain wisdom and insight into his greatness. Not that I thought that his brilliance would rub off on me and I would become a better writer, a more acknowledged national presence.

What I learned that night was that William Styron needs to pee on a regular basis, just like Sam or me. This is the great equalizer—the nitty-gritty bare-bones essential that brings us all together. All men need to pee, all humans and animals need to pee, and in this case I realize that although I may be, in contrast to Styron, an unknown, unrecognized writer, I am nevertheless better than him in one respect: I can pee at will.

As we sat in the emergency room that night in the local hospital where I had taken him for his medicine, chatting about the Clinton White House, Charles and Diana, and the other swell people with whom he hung out, I thought back to another pre-eminent author I had once hosted at a similar conference, the great Nelson Algren, author of the *Man with the Golden Arm*.

When he was asked what, if anything, he wanted to do during a free afternoon in Pittsburgh before his evening program began, he replied: "I need to buy some underwear."

Father Knows Best?

NOT LONG BEFORE we departed for Alaska, I was talking with a friend's son, a college sophomore, about what he would do after graduation. We were joking about whether his father would pay to send him to grad school. "My dad won't give me any more money after college," he said. "Grad school is out of the question, unless, of course, I pay."

"But your dad is always threatening to cut off your funding, and he never does. He gives you everything you ask for," I said.

We both laughed, for we knew what I said was true. My young friend, whom I will call Aaron, is spoiled. So is Sam. They get what they want—in excess, probably, of what they expect. But so what? They are both turning out to be nice boys, happy, relatively secure. The time for tough love and testing under life's searing fire is in the inevitable dark future. Someday, far too soon, neither Aaron's dad nor I will be around to safeguard and support our sons, so whatever we can do now, as far as I am concerned, is to the good. I will do almost anything to make Sam happy that isn't outrageous.

Perhaps I should be a sterner father, ruling with an iron fist, but brute force isn't my style. That is what my father did—punishing me for all of my misdeeds—sending me to bed without supper for not doing my chores or beating me with a strap when I talked back. I guess that is why I called my father, Jack R. Gutkind, "Jack the Ripper"— behind his back.

My ex-wife Patricia is constantly making fun of what a wimp I have become as a father to Sam. "Whatever happened to the old Lee?"

she inquires. Didn't the gang of thugs I hung out with in my twenties call me "The Cleat" because I was supposedly so mean that I would just as soon stomp my adversaries with my big black motorcycle boots than look at them? Didn't my students refer to me as "Steel Balls" when I first started teaching? Now I have become a pushover to a skinny, gangly adolescent, as has Aaron's dad, Alan, to his own son. Alan presents himself in real life as a grumpy Scrooge-like character. Except when it comes to his son.

Alan usually denies that he gives Aaron any extra money and is constantly threatening to cut him off and make him get a job and support himself. Despite his protestations, I figure Aaron can call all the shots for his future.

But then I had another thought, a semi-serious observation. "You may be right. Your father is very competitive," I told Aaron that day. "He may not want his son to have any more of an education than he does, so maybe he wouldn't pay for your grad school." Aaron looked at me quizzically.

"My parents both have masters degrees," he said.

"No they don't," I answered. "Your father never got an advanced degree."

"You're joking.

"No I'm not. He finished his course work and left town immediately thereafter. He never wrote his thesis."

Looking at Aaron's face fall, I could tell that what I said had totally shocked him. "Shut up," he said. "You're putting me on. I can't believe you."

The moment passed and we went on to other matters. But I couldn't help wondering why Alan would make himself so vulnerable by trying to get away with such an easily unveiled truth? And why, perhaps even more revealing and troublesome, would Alan so blatantly lie to himself?

I said to Sam—I made a point of this—"Sometimes you have to do or say things in your life that force you to mislead other people. Or you have to hold back and not say everything you know. But never lie," I said, "especially to someone you love. No matter how trivial or how far in the past it occurs, a lie will always come back and bite you. Like with Alan and Aaron so many years after the fact."

I think back on the moment I preached the no-lie mantra to Sam. So holier than thou, so self-righteous! And so embarrassing and lame, I now realize. Here's a better lesson: fathers should practice what they preach.

In many restaurants and hotels, the dividing line between childhood and adult is twelve years. Sometimes it's "children under twelve" or, more often, "children twelve and under," but either way, the price for Sam wherever we were increased—sometimes doubled—the moment he turned thirteen. But even though Sam had turned thirteen, he didn't seem to mind—outwardly—when I ordered food for him from the kids' menus at restaurants or requested a child's admission at museums and movies. I tried not to lie directly about this age, but even though I knew it was wrong, I did sometimes. "How old is your child?" the question would invariably be asked.

"Twelve."

I told myself that it was ok to tell a white lie and that Sam understood that the law was so arbitrary and unfair and that I worked hard for my money and that money doesn't grow on trees. While I understood rules, I couldn't seem to accept the idea of paying so much more for my child simply because an arbitrary day on a calendar had passed. Besides, no matter how tall he was getting, Sam was still a child, a mere baby, at least to me.

Sam usually didn't say anything during these transactions, but once, when I signed us up for a half-day Jeep tour in the San Juan mountains, the man at the registration desk asked him directly, "How old are you."

"Thirteen," Sam answered.

"Too bad," he said. "If you were twelve, your dad would have saved thirty-five dollars."

Those words were suddenly tattooed on my brain; *your dad would have saved thirty-five dollars*. While I have wasted thirty-five dollars — or three hundred and fifty dollars—more times than I could count, I couldn't let go of the idea that just one word from Sam, one change in a digit, equaled the cost of a half tank of gas for the Tundra.

Later, as we waited for the other people scheduled for this tour to arrive, I asked Sam why he didn't say he was twelve. "You cost me thirty-five dollars," I said. "You think money grows on trees?" I spoke softly, but he could tell I was angry and trying to hold my temper.

"Dad," he said, "you can lie for yourself, but I'm not going to lie for you."

I was immediately humiliated. From the beginning of our frequent father-and-son conversations, I had been moralizing to Sam about the importance of honesty. "Sometimes it is ok not to tell everyone everything you know, mostly for their own good or to protect others, say when people have told you things in confidence. But you never tell a lie. A lie will always comes back to haunt you."

Once, when Sam's Spanish teacher gave her students a surprise quiz and then wrote the answers on the blackboard and asked the students to grade each other, Ben, Sam's best friend, changed one of Sam's answers from wrong to right so that he could get an A. This was kind of Ben, a significant measure of loyalty and friendship, but wrong, and Sam knew it right away. He went to his teacher, reported Ben, and had his grade changed back to the B it deserved.

I was proud of Sam then and, although totally humiliated, proud of Sam now. His mom and I had done our work well. Sam was very honest, knew right from wrong, and had the courage to confront authority and endanger friendships and in the case of Ben, criticism from classmates, in order to do the right thing. But I couldn't say the same for myself.

Sam took the idea of being thirteen more seriously than I did. He didn't become bar mitzvah, as had I when I was thirteen, but he was more of a man now than I was then—or perhaps, if actions speak louder than words, more of a man that I am now, also.

The Rope Test

SAM HAS A GREAT sense of who and what he is—and who and what he is not. He knows that he is not wildly popular socially and that fact never really bothered him until, perhaps, he became a senior in high school, when being social becomes a real priority. Mostly, he doesn't desire or require constant attention from and interaction with his peers; his interests lie elsewhere. He has always been grounded—secure with his own identity.

I, on the other hand, fought for years to find myself, searching and searching to figure out who and what I was. I like to think I've come a long way, but I'm not quite there yet. I continue to search, to challenge myself and to find myself, different parts of me, as I come together as an adult. At thirteen, I was totally lost, but by the time of my eighteenth birthday, I was on a lifetime quest for self-discovery, beginning with my first character-building challenge and success: the rope test.

"I'm standing in an abandoned aircraft hangar in the U.S. Coast Guard station on the tip of Cape May, New Jersey, in a line of fifty-five men," I tell Sam. "This is the defining story of my life," I explain, "the moment when I realized my own potential—what and who I could be in the world and what I needed to do, how I would live in the world, how I would make life work for me."

We were boys when we had come together three and a half months before, raw recruits from all over the United States, not too much older than Sam is as I tell him this story. But we had suffered through the U.S. Marine Corps–style obstacle course, through constant midnight hazing, through marching in the snow and rain until our feet were numb and sometimes bleeding and our fingers were frozen blue, and we had survived, most of us. A few of the men had fallen by the wayside, unable to withstand the emotional humiliation and physical abuse, and been mustered out. Now, to proceed from boot camp to our new life as enlisted men we were expected to pass what Chief Petty Officer O'Reilly was calling the "rope test."

The rope test was the culminating experience of our boot-camp training, proof that we had truly achieved a measure of fitness and readiness that would allow us to perform our duties as military personnel in a professional and respectable manner. This wasn't just a test, by the way; the rope test was a necessity. We were The Guard, the service designated to protect the coast from enemy infiltration. There were other ways of boarding an invading or otherwise suspicious ship, Chief O'Reilly had told us, but when a rope is the only answer, a Guardsman must be able to do it.

We were nervous as we stood waiting for the signal to proceed, all of us, but excited and optimistic. The ropes were cascading down from the sloped ceiling of the hangar, knotted here and there, swaying in the drafty building, teasing and tantalizing us. Passing the rope test meant that we would receive two weeks leave to go home and show off our uniforms and our svelte new bodies to family and friends and then report to our new postings. Some of us were being assigned to schools for further training, while most of us would be serving on buoy tenders or patrol boats along the Atlantic coast. Exciting stuff for young men in the 1960s, boys from the backwoods of Arkansas, New Mexico, Indiana, or industrial ghettos like Pittsburgh—just before the specter and threat of Vietnam.

I was especially anxious to make a triumphant journey home, for I had probably progressed both intellectually and physically more than almost anyone else in the company. First, I was one of the youngest men in Company Alpha 48, barely eighteen years old, having just squeaked out of high school in the bare bottom of the fifth-fifth of my graduating class. Most of the men were older than me, many of them college graduates. And I had been in horrendous shape, physically. Before I enlisted in the Coast Guard—the only service that would take me—I had tried the Marines, the Air Force, and the Navy, and they had all laughed! I weighed 220 pounds.

But in the Guard, I had lost forty pounds after just fourteen weeks—and was certainly as fit as I had ever been, having been forced to march around the compound endlessly, do thousands of push-ups and sit-ups, and run and dive maniacally through the obstacle course. In the Guard, I learned to work harder and eat less—and to take orders, perform menial tasks, nonstop. I was as ready as I have ever been in my entire life to achieve something that had been inconceivable to me barely four months before: the rope test, fifty feet straight up to glory and advancement.

Chief O'Reilly raised his whistle, counted to three, hesitated momentarily, and blew. From a ragged line at the other end of the hangar, we all raced like mad to our ropes, jumped up as high as possible, grabbed a knot, and started to climb. The screams and yells and groans of the men of Alpha 48 were all around me, echoing through the hollow hangar, as I began to put one hand up over another and pull myself skyward. I felt invigorated, completely consumed by the challenge of the experience, almost as if I was flying up the rope.

When Chief O'Reilly blew his whistle a second time, almost everyone in company Alpha 48 was hanging at the top rung of their ropes waving their fists and cheering triumphantly. There was just one lowly sailor, one dejected young man, flapping about halfway up the rope, breathing heavily, stunned and confused, like a dying fish. Then, as everyone watched, that sailor lost his grip and plunged to the ground.

Lying on his back he could see all of his fellow recruits, soon to become full-fledged sailors, looking down at him from the tops of their ropes, and he felt instantly humiliated. It was one of the lowest and most confusing moments of his life. He hadn't just failed by a few feet or a couple of seconds to get to the top of the rope. He hadn't come close. Like the player in a baseball game striking out on three pitches without lifting his bat or the boxer knocked out in the first round without throwing a punch, that ineffective impotent young man—that loser—was me.

I had suddenly descended from the highest and most confident and exhilarating period of my life to one of the lowest. But it was also, in retrospect, my most useful and character-shaping moment, as well. That day I began to understand what it takes to be successful, to overcome overwhelming odds and achieve what some people may deem unlikely or impossible. The difference between the men and women who make an impact and those who are paralyzed by feelings of impotence is in how they respond to humiliation and defeat. That's the special line of embarkation—the magic moment I am intending to teach to Sam. A few weeks later, I passed the rope test by climbing and descending, up and down, fast and nimble—twice.

Over the years, I have adopted two ideas—"slogans," if you wish, or "mantras"—that became guiding principles of my life. The first comes from a surgeon I met while doing research for my book, *Many Sleepless Nights*, who was talking with a patient waiting for an organ for transplant. Paraphrasing Winston Churchill's appeal to the British people in 1941 in the darkest days of the German Blitzkrieg, the surgeon told his patient: "Never give in, never give up. Never. Never. Never. Ever." The real quotation is a little different, but the meaning is the same: "Never give in, never give in. Never. Never. Never. Never. In nothing great or small, large or petty, never give in, except to convictions of honor and good sense." The patient managed to live a couple more days—until a heart became available for transplant. I lost touch with him after his surgery, but the message was clearly imprinted on my mind. I will never give in—and I will never forget how much I might achieve in my life if I continue to try. Not trying means capitulation.

The second slogan also came from my old motorcycle friend, Burt, who had battled depression—and who had attempted to commit suicide by slitting his wrists on the day of his marriage. Paramedics saved his life. Weeks later, I asked him how he was managing to project a positive image after all he had been through. He chanted for me the little song he heard in the suicide unit in the psychiatric facility where he had been under twenty-four-hour observation. The song was simple and relentless, and eerie to hear again and again, but the message, so clear and simple, struck home:

"Fall down nine times . . . get up ten."

This, quite simply, was my rope-test mantra. If there was a specific focus to my legacy to my son Sam, this idea was the bone and sinew, heart and soul of what I wanted to teach him, although there have been times, I have to admit, that Sam has been a better teacher of me than I of him.

The "Make My Day" Syndrome

IT'S BEEN NEARLY a week since we crossed the border back into the United States to follow the Alaskan part of the AlCan to Homer Spit. We've been busy, involved in a great many activities. Today, Sam and I are the fifth and sixth fishermen to arrive at the docks in the early morning for a day of halibut fishing. The brisk biting wind sends a frigid mist across the deck of our fishing boat as we clamber aboard. It's a thirty-five-foot cruiser—a small cabin with four seats in the rear and a pilot's chair up front, which means two of the passengers must stand outside in the cold, holding onto the rail for dear life as we thrash our way out to the fishing area. Sam and I are the last two to arrive, ten minutes late because I needed to stop twice for coffee on the road. I apologize to Sam for my addictions.

Three of our fishing companions are retired businessmen from Minnesota, each adorned in a golfing shirt and a baseball cap with an emblem of the Minnesota state bird, the common loon. I actually looked this up when I got back to our room at the end of the day. Their names were Bill, George, and Herb, and they reminded me of the three weird brothers Larry, Darryl, and Darryl on *Newhart*, a 1980s situation comedy on TV. The star, comedian Bob Newhart, helped his wife run a bed-and-breakfast in Vermont and also hosted a local TV Show. Larry, Darryl, and Darryl were neighbors who appeared periodically, mostly a set piece to introduce themselves. Larry was the spokesperson; the Darryls never talked. "My name is Larry," Larry would say whenever he entered the inn, "and this is my brother Darryl and this is my other brother Darryl." Then Newhart would give the camera an eye-rolling look and the laugh track would go on. The plot pretty much stopped there.

Herb, who was taller and perhaps a bit older, was the Larry of the Minnesota contingent. He said: "My name is Herb—and this is Bill and this is George." Their mission: to bring home halibut for their families and friends to enjoy for the rest of the year—and to not talk or look at anyone else except each other for the rest of this boat trip. This is their third or fourth season in a row, fishing for food in Kachemak Bay.

This information I gathered from eavesdropping as we stood at the entryway to the cabin, for they were the most unfriendly folks I had ever met—or not met, actually, since the two Darryls looked right through me, no response, when I said hello. The Canadians we talked with on the AlCan, and most Alaskans we ran into, wherever, tended to be open to conversation. But these Minnesotans reminded me of the woman border guard in Portal: they all three stared at my earring, as if the blue turquoise nugget tainted me. "Nice morning," I said to them, with as much bravado and cheerfulness as I could muster, just to see if they would respond.

Herb nodded. Darryl and the other Darryl stared at the water. They could have offered to move over and squeeze at least one of us—Sam was the smallest—onto the bench seat in the cabin, but they didn't. Eventually, Sam would make them give up at least one of their seats—quite willingly—but that story comes later. All told, the Minnesota Darryls transformed halibut fishing into a funeral march. But then all of this scintillating conversation ceased as the engine was fired up. We ended up on the outside rather than in the cabin, immediately freezing to death in the early dawn Alaskan air, while the bouncing boat was shaking our stomachs inside out.

I confess, I am not exactly certain what makes halibut fishing or any kind of fishing so popular—we were not having fun right then—except for the fact that you get a lot of fish (or meat) for a relatively small effort and investment. But that's practical—not fun. Fishing for salmon (coho) is more fun, I am told—and better eating—but the season for salmon is limited while halibut is nearly a year-round activity, weather permitting, although the best halibut fishing is May through September.

I sometimes, long ago, accompanied my old deer-hunting buddies, Randy and Larry, when they went bottom fishing for carp in the

Monongahela River at the edge of the Homestead Steel Works. Swimming through the sludge and waste of Andrew Carnegie's old mills, these fish were old, fat, covered in black tar-like oil and waste, and totally inedible. But Randy caught dozens of these fat carp to use for fertilizer to grow marijuana. When we went deer hunting we smoked this stuff, which Larry called Tasmanian Bunko Weed—not for any reason I could understand. Curiously, the sludge in the fish totally masked any telltale odor of dope.

Once late at night, at the northernmost tip of the Allegheny National Forest in Pennsylvania, when we were out spotlighting deer, the local sheriff pulled us over because Larry, sucking on a Tasmanian Bunko Weed joint, was driving erratically. For a moment we thought we were going to be in big trouble, especially out there in the boonies, but when the sheriff asked us what were doing out so late (looking for deer in the dark and making them freeze by shining a blinding light into their eyes was illegal), Larry said, "Night fishing." The sheriff nodded vehemently as he sniffed inside the car: "You don't have to tell me," he said, "I can smell it." It was actually never clear to us what he smelled, but we took it to mean the carp rather than the Bunko Weed, which was the reason he let us go.

Fishing didn't turn me on, except when Larry brought along his Bunko Weed, but I also can't say why killing Bambi—or trying to kill Bambi—was exciting, either. But deer hunting is a sacred blue-collar tradition in western Pennsylvania and a rite of passage for kids growing up there, not unlike a bar mitzvah. You join the men on "First Monday"—that's the Monday after Thanksgiving, usually the first Monday in December—when you are old enough to get a license, which is twelve in Pennsylvania, where two hundred thousand white-tailed deer are harvested annually. From a sportsman's point-of-view, you do not *kill* deer; rather, you "harvest" the biggest and oldest animals because of a dearth of vegetation in the forest for the multiplying whitetail herd to consume. Bucks—male deer with antlers, which hunters call "bone"—are the object of the hunt on first Monday. By eliminating the big strong male who, due to size, strength, and experience, controls the food supply, the lives of younger, weaker members of the herd, who might otherwise starve, are, theoretically, spared.

The procedure in deer hunting is to sneak into the woods in the dark at about four in the morning, conceal yourself—some hunters climb trees—and wait, often in sub-zero temperatures, for first light when the deer wake up and start foraging for food. You need to sit very still so as not to give yourself away, and to be down-wind of your prey, because deer are very sensitive to smell and sound—and wait with your trigger finger ready. The philosophy in deer hunting is total ambush. When you ambush your first unsuspecting deer and kill it, you are considered a man.

I have yet to make that passage into deer-hunting manhood. On first Monday, I would usually wait for first light and then, if there were no deer directly in my line of fire, I would soon get anxious or bored, get up (or climb down if I was in a tree) and walk around, looking for other hunters to talk with. Walking along the side of a road one first Monday, I met a woman hauling a seven-point (the number of antlers or "bone" on a buck) in the bed of her pick-up truck. She shot the buck in the left temple—she shoved her pinky finger into the tiny hole below the animal's eye to show me—a single shot from her 30-06 at a hundred yards, she said (deer hunters have a keen sense of distance). In the field where the deer lay dead, she slit open it's stomach with a Buck knife, pulled out its innards, lashed its bone with a rope, and then dragged it along the ground to her truck. At home, she would hang the deer from the supporting beam of her front porch so that at the end of the day, when her neighbors rode by in their pick-up trucks, they'd witness her success.

The closest I came to harvesting my own deer, I was literally so close I could hear him panting. I was in a tree, hovering right above him. Slowly, carefully, I concentrated. Focus. Visualize, I said to myself. Raising my rifle, I was ready to squeeze-off. And then, suddenly, for no reason I could easily explain, except that maybe, deep down inside, I didn't really want to kill Bambi, I lost my composure—and I yanked on the trigger. I fired; the sound deafening, pounded my ears. I kept on shooting wildly, though I couldn't see the animal at whom I was supposed to be aiming, couldn't see where the bullets were going, either. I'd lost it—everything. Awareness, rationality, balance. I fell apart. Then I felt myself slipping down from the tree. Losing my grip. Bullets flying. Loud explosions. Feeling myself falling, like a flag, unfurling and gyrating. I punched the ground with my body, my head smacked against the tree. I suffered a concussion, and when I could finally think straight again, which took a couple of weeks, at least, I decided that deer hunting was not for me.

Fishing could be less harrowing—at least that's what I thought, until I realized, when the Minnesota Darryls forced us out of the cabin and out onto that bare, cold, bouncing deck, that fishing could be even more challenging—and traumatic.

EARLIER IN THE WEEK, on Kachemak Bay, we had stopped to watch the fishing boats coming in on the long dock connecting the town of

Homer to Homer Spit, the furthest tip of the peninsula. One halibut had been caught by a woman in her twenties. It weighed 102 pounds and was bigger than Sam.

"Was it a fight?" I asked her.

"I had the help of three strong men," she said. "The challenge was dragging it into the boat. We almost had to shoot him—or lose the boat—and the fish."

Shooting halibut in order to keep your boat in one piece is par for the course, according to my friend and former student Kathy Tarr, who worked as a fish-slimer when she arrived here thirty-five years ago. "We cleaned fish on an assembly line. Everyone had a job in the process. I scraped off the green slime between the flesh and the skin in a straight line with a tablespoon, as the fish, on a conveyor belt, came by. It was disgusting work—raw and smelly. You lived for the end of the day so that you could go home, dive into a hot bath, and wash the stink off."

That "stink" is part of Alaska—as is "washing it off." Whatever mistakes you have made in the lower 48, mean very little here in the new frontier. It's a wild, real experience that allows you to redefine yourself and redirect the course of your life. "In a way," she says, you leave the "stink of your life" behind, and if you are working as a slimer, replace it with something awful—but more defined. It could also lead to a better life, one of achievement and adventure.

Kathy graduated from Florida State University and went to work in a bookstore there. That's where she discovered John McPhee's best selling book about Alaska, *Coming into the Country*. She devoured the book, and soon after, when her boyfriend, who worked for the Federal Aviation Administration, was transferred to Alaska, she followed for a two-week visit. "I never went home." This is not an unfamiliar story. She raised a family and launched a career as a writer and teacher over the subsequent thirty years.

Later that second morning, we walked the beach with Kathy and a few friends we'd met at the conference, kicking the stones and dodging the tangled driftwood on the shore. This is not a typical beach—no smooth sand for baking in the sun. Rugged and rocky, it's majestic and larger than life, with snow-capped mountains in the distance separated by the icy blue Kachemak Bay, all of it spellbinding in its vastness and kaleidoscope of colors. This morning was especially clear and brilliant. There was a misty scrim of pearl white clouds hovering across the bay where the water met the beach.

Michele, who came to Alaska seven years ago "because a friend was driving there and I had nothing else to do that week," manages a bar in Seward. She's a refugee from Berkeley, California—her father is a producer for PBS there, she said, as she discussed her partner, Jim, a dichotomy. "He's an environmental activist and a logger."

Native Alaskans are entitled, one time, to ten thousand board feet of lumber free, to build a house, she said. Jim felled the trees and had them cut and milled, with the help of friends. But according to Martha, whom I met in a bar, Alaskans are forever starting to build houses and hardly ever finishing them. They get the wood—anything for free—but then they have to do the work, which is another matter entirely. "The work is not free—it costs them pain and effort and suddenly the wood don't seem worthwhile."

Fish, too, seem abundant. "We're forever giving fish away," Kathy said. "Everybody's got too much fish, but it's great fun to fight those mothers and pull them in. You feel on top of the world—like a pioneer or a frontiersman, gathering food for your family. It's real primal satisfaction! Some folks in Alaska live for the fishing," she adds. "Nothing else matters. Without fishing, they would die."

Which was a perfect description of our fourth companion on the boat that morning. Unlike the three hostile graying Minnesota men in their baseball loon caps, Galen was a native Alaskan, born and bred.

Galen was grizzled, dark, weather-beaten, and unshaven. The four fingertips on his right hand were missing, casualties of frostbite and runaway chainsaws, common occurrences here. Galen carried his own fishing equipment aboard—rod, reel, and tackle (the rest of us were using the ship's gear), and he talked nonstop with Sean, the captain of the boat, about fishing: where he had been, what he had caught, where he intended to go next, and what he expected to catch. Galen went on and on in a lazy, flat-affect drawl, even when Sean wasn't paying attention; Galen didn't seem to care if anyone listened or understood exactly what he was saying or what body of water he was referring to. Galen, as Kathy had described, was one of those who were truly obsessed.

"Is that what you do, kind of travel around and fish for halibut and salmon, from place to place?" I asked Galen. I posed this question before the engines were fired and we began thrashing our way to the fishing area; once we got underway, it was too loud and choppy to talk—or think. I was actually wondering how he supported himself, in between his fishing expeditions. That was the genus of my question.

Galen nodded gravely and, as if I had uttered something deadly serious, he pondered for a long time, his four chipped fingers, stroking the dirty stubble on his chin. Then he shook his head slowly up and down and took a deep breath. "Is there anything else," he finally said, "than fishing?"

He uttered those words softly, in a grave and contemplative manner, almost as if he was sharing with me the profound secret of his life. Perhaps he was.

THIS KIND OF machismo rhetoric fascinates me. I call it the "Make my day" syndrome. This phrase is from *Sudden Impact*, one of the Dirty Harry series of movies, in which Clint Eastwood—Harry—points his Smith & Wesson .44 magnum at a thug in a restaurant who's holding a waitress at gunpoint. Harry and the thug eyeball each other for a while as the thug contemplates shooting the waitress or making a run for it. Which is when Harry, who has already killed most of the thug's henchmen, says to the thug the immortal words: "Go ahead. Make my day." The thug relents, thereby demonstrating Harry's coolness under pressure and showing that only a few words can sum up everything necessary sometimes—no matter how complicated. Harry's persona says it all, like the country (Alaska, the Rocky Mountain west, etc.) is so vast and beautiful that you can let the sights and situations speak symbolically—let the land and the sky determine the meaning of everything. Words enhance rather than contain the message.

But it is not just in the far west where, as the song "Home on the Range" goes, "Seldom is heard a discouraging word, and the skies are not cloudy all day," but any place where men play their macho thing. In New York, Marlon Brando tells Robert Duvall in "The Godfather" to "make him [an adversary] an offer he can't refuse." The meaning is more than clear in context. And when asked why he wants to risk his life to go down an untamed river in a raft in the movie "Deliverance," the lead character, played by Burt Reynolds replies, "Because it's there."

I am not saying I buy into this "make my day" syndrome. I don't want to do something ill advised and unnecessary simply because it happens to be there. George W. Bush once taunted Al Qaeda and the Taliban on national television with a wave of his arm and the challenge to "Bring it on!" He got more than he bargained for, though, and he backed away from this rhetoric a few years later. But the idea of symbolic minimalist expression is infectious and comforting; it makes basic communications easier—and sometimes very effective. Why be articulate if you can more easily say something in a few words that represent a myriad of ideas and responses—and make the speaker look more manly and erudite in the process?

But even the women here in Alaska ooze machismo in word and deed—unlike anything in the east or midwest. On the ferry *Columbia*, which Sam and I took for four days along the Alaskan intercoastal waterway, we met Willow and Jean, who got off at Ketchikan during a five-hour layover for a walk up a nearby nature trail at the edge of town. We were following what Alaskans call the "Inside Passage" along the Alaskan Marine Highway, beginning in Juneau and wandering through Skagway and the Tongass National Forest before finally ending at Bellingham, Washington.

Five minutes up a hill, heading to a small lake above Ketchikan, they ran into a bear. "I could almost touch him," Jean said. Without thinking, she turned her back and began to walk rapidly in the opposite direction. Willow suddenly grabbed her by the shoulders and whirled her back around. "What are you doing?" she said.

"Getting away from the bear."

Intellectually, Jean was aware of a bear's dangerous chase response—instantly pursuing anything that seemed to fear it. Cornered by a bear, you should talk loudly, yell, move your arms rapidly, wave or jump. Never retreat or show your back. That's the Alaskan way to deal with danger, not just bears but the general hostility of the world at large. Jean had heard the advice a dozen times, but the sudden sight of the bear near Ketchikan, almost within touching distance, had spooked her.

Willow was a nurse who has lived the past fifteen years in the Alaskan backcountry. A tall, middle-aged woman with a jagged scar on her chin, she had worked in the backwoods as a guide and as a deckhand. She was not one to be easily spooked. Now she was heading for Nevada City, California, to start a new life. I asked her how she got her scar, but with the exception of shrugging her shoulders and smiling wanly and the cryptic phrase, "Oh, how it happened!" she wasn't about to provide information. But "Oh, how it happened!" said a lot.

"I'll bet it was from a bear," Jean speculated. Willow declined to answer.

Joan, another woman I talked with, was a former professional wrestler and rodeo bronc rider. She was traveling—looking for something "I don't think I will find," she said. "You either take to the life here or you don't, and then you move on." That was the extent of her "make my day/home on the range" declaration. At that moment, it sounded profound.

Even those who initially take to the life, like Willow, are often worn out after a half dozen years and retreat back to the lower 48 for shelter and survival. The bears in Alaska are symbolic; they represent the overall hardship of the state—and the awesome stress of the experience of living there.

"Never turn your back to a bear," Willow whispered to Jean that afternoon as she whirled Jean back around and forced her to face the bear down.

The advice must have been pretty good because when Jean turned back and looked the bear in the eye, the bear checked both of them out and then casually ambled away.

"Glad you were around," Jean told Willow as they related the story to Sam and me, back on the boat. "You knew exactly what to do. You had the situation well under control."

"Usually I carry my control on my hip," said Willow. "But this time it was buried in the bottom of the trunk of my car."

"On your hip?" I asked.

"A .44 Ruger magnum," she said. "The Ruger is my great equalizer."

This was the "make my day" syndrome to perfection.

There are, of course, contradictions to all of these stereotypes. Randy and Larry, my two hunting buddies, as strong and rugged-looking as was Galen, were hairdressers. Once, sitting in a bar the night after first Monday, celebrating their buck kills, a bartender asked Larry and Randy what they did for a living. "We're beauticians," Randy said.

"My ass," the bartender replied.

It was another "make my day" declaration.

The Red Bike

THE WRITERS' CONFERENCE here in Alaska collects an eclectic mix of attendees, some of whom don't necessarily intend to be writers or know what a writer's life is all about. "I'm curious about writing," Martha told me. "I've lived a lot of life. I have something to say to people."

"That's what writing is all about," I tell her, "communicating to readers, making an impact."

It's the last night of the conference, the night before our halibut fishing trip, and the keynote conference speaker, Maxine Hong Kingston, is talking about peace. She is not talking about peace in the way writers need peace and quiet in order to write something significant. She is talking about peace on earth and goodwill to men. Peace in the world. Peace in our time. She sneers at the *New York Times* for taking her to task for giving her last book a maudlin happy ending. "What's wrong with happy endings?" she wants to know. "We should all write books with happy endings." Not if you want it to seem real, I think.

"What did you think of the story she told?" Michele, whose boyfriend was the logger and activist, asked me.

"It was haunting and memorable, although I'm not certain it rings true."

"It may well be true," says Martha, "but it doesn't sound right."

"Something about her delivery," says Kathy. "Flat. There's no eye contact."

Maxine Hong Kingston's father has died and she goes to the funeral. Then she drives home and, as she gets closer to her home, the smoke and the pandemonium caused by an onrushing forest fire becomes more evident, and she begins to understand that her home may not be there any more. Her world might be on the edge of extinction. She parks her car, somehow manages to evade the fire and law enforcement authorities and makes her way on foot back to her house, which, she comes to realize, is no longer there. It is gone. Charred ash. Burned to the bone. All of her possessions are gone, including the manuscript for her next book, *The Fourth Book of Peace*.

She doesn't say how she feels at this moment about the loss of her book—or for that matter about the loss of her father. Her presentation is oddly passive and ambivalent, as if it has happened to someone else, and she is reporting the story, as if she is a newscaster on TV.

I don't know how long Maxine Hong Kingston stood staring at the charred remains of her house, but then she suddenly saw a man on a red bicycle. He stopped to chat for a while, about what, we don't know. She doesn't tell us. What has happened regarding the fire, no doubt, and how they feel, was our best guess, the obvious assumption. Eventually the man on the red bicycle offers her a ride. So she jumps on the handlebars of the red bike and the man peddles her back to her car.

Maxine Hong Kingston is short and slight, with long and strikingly dramatic silver hair. If you listen intently to the sound of her voice or get close enough to peer into her smoky blue eyes, she establishes a mystical and memorable presence.

Later in her long and wide-ranging talk, she will tell us of her trip to Washington with many other women writers, to confront the White House's shock-and-awe tactics at the start of the Iraq War—the women all dressed in pink to enhance their femininity and solidify their message of peace.

But right now, the image of this woman, whose father was lost, whose home and possessions were lost, including the book to which she had devoted two years of her life, riding on the handlebars of a red bike through smoldering ruins, remains with me. The images come together.

I think that her story of riding on the handlebars of a red bike peddled by a perfect stranger in the middle of a massive forest fire that killed twenty-four people is a ridiculous image—bizarre—and probably not totally faithful to the reality of the experience, and yet, I do not disbelieve her. Stories have a tendency to be skewed by time and circumstance. But telling details are also indelible and overwhelming to the storyteller. Having her possessions—the very evidence of her life—being so suddenly destroyed somehow allows the bizarre and unusual to shine through. The man on the red bike and the hitching of a ride on his handlebars is unlikely, but it is what she remembers: The tangible kernel that signifies the intangible and unexpected heartache of the moment, resulting in the message of optimism and despair that emanated from that story. Balanced precariously on the handlebars of a stranger's red bike, crushed from loss and stunned with emptiness, her book gone, it was at that point, she told her audience, "I realized that I still had my ideas."

I thought about this the following morning when I met Galen on the fishing boat. There is so much that can be said sometimes with so few words, as I have noted. Maxine Hong Kingston mastered the moment and captured the spirit of the writer and the writing life, all in five words. Whatever loss she suffered, whatever pain and emptiness she experienced, "I still had my ideas."

Another famous writer, Tom Wolfe, author of the *Electric Kool Aid Acid Test* and the *Bonfire of the Vanities*, once responded to an editor for Esquire Magazine who wanted him to write a brief description of an event he had witnessed, "I don't have time to write it short." So, too, with Maxine Hong Kingston: her hour-long presentation had nevertheless led to a precious nugget of crystallized clarity.

While writing it or saying it short is sometimes most effective, there are, of course, many instances when keeping information to yourself is the best approach of all. This would have been my best approach to Sam's toast-buttering process—of that I am certain. And, as it turned out, silence was my best approach to barfing on the boat. I played that story well.

STANDING OUTSIDE in the rear of the boat for more than a stomach-jarring hour, holding on to a rail for dear life as the boat bounced and rolled, its bow crashing repeatedly every fifteen seconds or so into the oncoming whitecaps, was, for Sam and me, the least of our problems. The challenge had nothing to do with fishing or holding on; it was, rather, in not turning green and, certainly more important, if and when we did turn green, not barfing all over each other.

Sam was straightforward and clear as time passed. "I'm getting sick," he said. "I'm going to throw up."

"That's too bad," I said. "Hold it down."

"I'm afraid I won't be able to."

"You have to," I told him.

"I can't," he said.

"You have no choice," I told him.

This is the kind of conversation that Sam hates, for he expects me, his father, to fix things whenever he has problems or to, at the least, provide answers that are palatable. When he was younger, his problems were more easily dealt with and he had less of an idea of what I needed to do or what he wanted me to do to satisfy him. Sometimes simple consolation was enough to make him happy. And, as a buffer, he was often unaware of the consequences of his dilemma, when I couldn't help him more directly and immediately. But now he realized that the eminent result of increasing nausea was tossing his cookies, and although he also realized he was helpless to do anything about it, he expected me, his father, to come up with a solution—fast.

The typical male response in situations like this, when pain or sickness are inevitable, is to suck it up, in silence. Endure. That's what men do, I have often told him. Which is exactly what I was doing at that very moment—I was in a similar situation. I too was becoming increasingly nauseous and dizzy; it was all I could do to hold onto the rail, to stay inside the boat, and smile, while making sure that Sam was, if not comfortable, then, at the least, secure.

But I did not want to give myself away to Sam, first because I couldn't easily lecture him about the necessity of holding it in, fighting and enduring, which is what men do, while I lost all control and tossed my cookies. And, in fact, I couldn't actually afford to toss my cookies, which would mean letting go of Sam who was, at the moment, becoming increasingly vulnerable. Who will take care of Sam while I am barfing my brains out, hanging over the side of the boat? Not those somber silent Darryls from Minnesota.

Galen was a better bet, but only under emergency conditions. I could feel my stomach churning, with everything inside of me moving upward and converging in my throat, but I refused to let it happen, no matter how seemingly inevitable, until Sam was safe.

Suddenly Sam could take it no more and began keeling over. "I'm getting dizzy," he said.

As his knees buckled, I caught him by the waist, dragged him into the cabin and confronted the Minnesotans. "My son is sick," I yelled. "You have to give him some space to sit down—or suffer the consequences." I pushed him directly toward the bench seat they were occupying.

Suddenly, the Minnesotans woke up. The Darryls moved quickly, making room on the seat—and just in time. I knew that Sam was on the verge of exploding. Holding onto him with one hand, I grabbed the white barf bucket with my other hand and shoved it in front of his face. Later, with Sam safe on the bench, wedged in beside Galen, I crept around to the other side of the boat and barfed over the rail in secrecy, maintaining my manly facade.

Hakuna Matata

Africa—July 2009

THE INTERNATIONAL BICYCLE FUND, or Ibike, a nonprofit organization based in Seattle and devoted to nonmotorized transportation, had promised a unique experience—"fascinating visits to development projects, national parks, traditional villages," according to its website. This was exactly what Sam and I had wanted: to explore somewhere new and exotic, to stretch ourselves physically, to immerse ourselves in a part of the world about which we knew very little—and to have one last adventure before Sam started college.

We began with three days on Zanzibar Island, fifteen miles across the Indian Ocean from Tanzania's capital, Dar es Salaam, where we explored historic Stone Town, sailed to Prison Island, famous for its gigantic turtles, and went on an interesting half-day bus "Spice Tour." But all eight members of our group had traveled thousands of miles and paid the robber-baron airlines anywhere from $100–$265 per bike for one-way transport, so we were anxious to start riding.

Although our ages ranged from eighteen to sixty-eight, we shared a desire to travel on two wheels, to make a more direct connection with the land and the people, and to exert strength and energy—and sometimes sweat and tears—toward that end. "I don't want to see Africa from a windshield," Chris Maier, a policy planner from Alexandria, Virginia, said. Ibike and our guide, Jerome, had promised a course that would get us to the bone and sinew of the heartland, where tourists rarely ventured. And the first couple of days in the lush Usambara Mountains, the "Switzerland of Tanzania," where the biking began, fulfilled that promise.

Lushoto, the main town in the Usambara District, is famous for its production of vegetables and spices, evidenced in the sprawling marketplace we passed through while hiking to the Irente Children's Home, an orphanage in the Usambara Highlands. The African marketplace doubles as a vast dollar store for clothes, furniture, and small appliances. We bought diapers and baby formula and a few toys for the kids—mostly infants and toddlers from families decimated by AIDS or poverty.

Though Lushoto is a relatively developed area, the contrast between the traditional lifestyle and the emerging new world is sometimes stunning. The day we visited the orphanage a suspected burglar was chased through town by neighbors and caught and beaten on the main street while the police watched impassively.

Around Lushoto many children knew English. Mostly they wanted to "high five" with us and respond to our traditional "hello" in Swahili ("Jambo") by showing off and replying to us surprised "mzungus" (foreigners), "Good afternoon."

As we ventured deeper into the interior, children would emerge everywhere, staring at us with intense curiosity, but from a distance—at least temporarily. Jo Spenser, an elementary school teacher in Dubai, was our Pied Piper. A striking woman with long blonde hair, she used sign language and a few basic words of English to organize little songs, which some of the children would sing with her. She also began taking pictures with her digital camera and showing the children their images—which excited and intrigued them. Wary adults would also emerge for picture taking. When I explained to one man that I could not give him his photo, he asked, "You put me in there. Why can't you take me out?"

More unique than digital cameras to villagers were our flashy modern bikes with their knobby tires, padded seats, panniers, and a plethora of gears. Jo and Chris Maier and Chris Pell, a banker from the UK, rode well-equipped mountain bikes, while Chris's wife, Emma Pell, had a good street-bike outfitted with mountain-bike tires. Sam and I and Jim Merchant, a research scientist from Raleigh, North Carolina, and his wife Shoshana Serxner, a retired librarian, were not so well prepared.

Considering the cost to ship bikes, Ibike founder David Mozer had recommended that we buy used bikes and leave them in the country. Previous participants had purchased old bikes for under $150. The

Merchants tried this, but Jim, a former motorcycle mechanic, was in constant repair mode. Sam and I had bought new inexpensive Diamondback mountain bikes for under $200 from Dick's Sporting Goods. Late one afternoon on the third day out, Sam fishtailed in the sand and fell over. His new bike literally fell apart.

Asking around, we learned that there was a bike mechanic in the next village, but we couldn't figure out how to get Sam's bike there—until we spotted a man with a motorcycle and Chris Pell came up with a plan to hire him. I sat behind the motorcyclist and balanced Sam's bike on my lap. When we took off down the narrow rock-strewn dirt road, swerving unsteadily, I realized that there was a good chance I would never see my traveling companions and my son again—or at least not while I was in one piece.

These spontaneous annoyances and adventures were what made this trip so troublesome—and simultaneously exciting and compelling. Jerome was cooperative and helpful, though stretched, without an assistant. But we adjusted to the problems and laughed at the inconveniences, adapting to the theme of African optimism we encountered everywhere. "Hakuna matata," the people would say. "No problem."

One of the most taxing yet delightful days occurred between Mtae, the destination after Lushoto, and Ndugnu. Jerome led us into a tiny village to hire a guide to show us a short-cut through the thorn-filled Mkomasi plains to a picturesque river bank at a bridge that would be perfect for lunch—an hour away, Jerome promised. After one man volunteered, a number of others swarmed Jerome begging for the job. Jerome decided to stay with the original volunteer. In the end we found the spot by the river—three hours later. Our guide had gotten lost. But we had a terrific lunch. "Hakuna matata," we said.

There were very few modern facilities in the places we stayed—no television, running water, or flush toilets in many of these "guest" houses. Mostly we were given buckets. Water was available from a lone spigot in the room or delivered to our doors—sometimes hot and more often cold. Breakfasts of eggs and bread and local fruit were usually satisfying. We grabbed lunch in villages along the way. Dinner was sparse and rarely nourishing. But Coca Cola was available almost everywhere, as were Kilimanjaro and Tusker Beers, which kept us going.

While sharing beers one night at a "guest" house in Ndungu, we met a man who said he was a Catholic priest, and two of his students. The men were friendly as they discussed God and religion—perhaps, we thought later, too friendly, especially with Jo and Emma. When we turned in, we wondered why there were so many slightly morose women sitting in one large room adjacent to the bar, until we heard later the blaring music and the peals of laughter, a racket that continued all night. We realized that this "guest" house was a brothel.

The forty-four-mile ride from Ndungu to Same, was the longest and most difficult, over a hazardous roller-coaster washboard road of dirt and clay. We dodged thorns sharp enough to slice tires, sand piles, and jagged rocks under an intense and beating sun. It was slow going and agonizingly painful, even with padded biking shorts. We prayed for a paved road—even a flat dirt road. We didn't see much asphalt during the week-long ride until the second to last day, the day Sam crashed. He was on a paved two-lane highway. which may well be the reason he lost concentration and was cavalier about his speed.

PART II

Religious Experiences

Laowai

Tibet—March 2008

THE *RAT-TAT-TAT* OF gunfire awoke me. It was just a single burst—a rapid, thundering slash into the silent darkness. I was out of bed and fumbling with the curtains at the window in an instant.

I had heard that same disruptive sound earlier that night, and had assumed, half-asleep, that it was simply a car backfiring. But then as I lay there, the tense events of the afternoon played back in my mind:

The Jokhang Temple, the spiritual center of Tibet, usually surrounded by waves of prostrating pilgrims, suddenly closing as we were about to enter; the shopkeepers and street vendors packing up their merchandise in the popular Barkhor marketplace surrounding the Temple during the height of the market day; the police in their loose-fitting green and khaki, emblazoned with bold red stripes and lettering, suddenly appearing; then the soldiers in dull brown emerging out of the shadows, their stern, wary eyes lazering the streets; and our guide, Tenzin, his bronze, sharp-featured face tightening with tension, announcing softly, but insistently, "We must go. Now."

We walked rapidly for fifteen or twenty minutes, following Tenzin, who was communicating with our driver, Chamba, by cell phone. Chamba, in our Landcruiser, was blocked from entering certain streets, so we had to keep walking, chasing Tenzin's back and his quick jerky strides, as he zigged and zagged through alleys and winding, narrow partially-paved side streets, his cell phone glued to his ear, until he and Chamba could devise a rendezvous plan.

"Dad? What's happening?" Sam asked.

"I will tell you in the car," Tenzin interjected. But even after our rendezvous with Chamba, Tenzin tactfully avoided providing substantial information. There was a "one-land" demonstration further down in the Barkhor, some blocks from where we were, Tenzin told us. "It has to do with the D.L.," he said.

"You mean the Dalai Lama?" I asked.

Tenzin nodded without responding directly to my question. "Ears are everywhere," Tenzin said. Since the Han occupation, Tibetans did not speak the name of their Priest and King, head of the Monastic Hierarchy of Buddha, out loud, he informed us.

That evening, the streets around our hotel were cordoned off. Gaunt Chinese men in cheap black suits and wrinkled white shirts milled on corners and in doorways, chain smoking cigarettes and talking softly, glancing at us, as we walked up Beijing Middle Road toward the Tibetan Steak House. We intended to eat yak steak and blood soup on our first night in Lhasa. "We'll be yakking it up," Sam said.

We had already sampled yak butter tea, a warm, oily concoction of tea, sugar, butter, and salt at the home of an old lady Tenzin had introduced us to, who lived in a neat hut in a rock-strewn alley in the middle of Lhaza. The old lady had served us a number of Tibetan delicacies, a few of which Sam had sampled. At home Sam remained a conservative eater over the years, difficult to please, but lately, on the road, he could let go and experiment. Slumping on a quilted bench and sipping the warm, oily yak tea brew, he allowed the old lady's filthy cat to jump up on his lap, and he stroked it gingerly. The old lady, her face a coppery tan, continued to smile and stare at Sam.

Tall and lanky, Sam had been a curiosity the moment we landed in Tibet. His narrow shoulders and smooth white face framed with light brown hair loomed like a mast over the crushing waves of dark, short Tibetans and Chinese, who consistently whispered the word for foreigner—*laowai*—as we walked by. Sam was unaware that he was attracting attention; he is often oblivious to his surroundings.

The Tibetan Steak House was closed, an accordion of sheet metal rolled over the door and front windows—airtight—as were most of the other businesses on Beijing Middle Road. Our neighborhood was in the heart of the Han district, and the tension and anger—and fear—were thick in the air. We joined a dozen westerners back at our hotel, in a nearly empty restaurant.

"What is happening out in the streets?" I asked a young Tibetan man—a student—who had been having dinner with friends and volunteered to help translate the menu.

"You will find out tomorrow," he said. His voice was bursting with restrained excitement. "No one will talk with you now," he added softly. And then in a whisper: "Tomorrow will be a beautiful day."

All of this came back to me as I lay in bed after the first burst of gunfire, dead tired from the flight into Lhasa from Chengdu in China's Szechuan Province the day before where I had been teaching and touring with Sam, and the shocking adjustment to the altitude here in the snow-capped Himalayas, from 500 meters in China (1,640 feet) to 3600 meters (12,000 feet) in less than two hours. But I was on edge, unable to succumb to the sleep I desperately needed.

So when the sound came a second time, the jarring, unnatural crack and pop of gunfire, that haunting, threatening *rat-tat-tat*, I knew that whatever was happening in Tibet on this night was much more than a minor, temporary disturbance. Something serious—life threatening—was taking place in this country and to its people—and perhaps to me and to my son.

I ripped open the curtains and saw the soldiers illuminated in the streetlights, marching rapidly, equipped with riot gear—full-body shields, bamboo batons, and automatic weapons, and heading in our direction.

And then I thought, as I sank into the chair next to the window and peered across the darkened room at the long sinewy shape of my beloved son, bundled under his blankets, so peacefully sleeping, unaware and innocent of all of the angry, violent commotion outside: "What have I done to him *this* time?"

That was 6 months before Kilimanjaro.

Creation Elation

OUR FIRST REAL truckin' destination back in 2003, during the era of the wet run and the Ranger, was the Grand Canyon, where, I told Sam, he would see such a sight that he could truly conceive of the notion that, if not God, then something really extraordinary—out of this world—actually existed. I said this half jokingly, although when I first visited the Canyon I was, like many people, overpowered by the pure magnificence of it all. How could such an overwhelming sight have been created by pure accident of nature? And if so, who created— what was—nature? These questions are not unique to me; many have pondered such riddles in a much more sophisticated manner. But truly, I had really never given God any thought whatsoever. God, to me, when I was young, was connected to religion, which, I thought, was kind of a crock. If it wasn't for religion I wouldn't have had to go to Hebrew School after regular school every afternoon from three-thirty to six, studying for my bar mitzvah, Monday through Thursday. I could have been playing softball with my friends. If not for religion, I would not have to wear a suit and sit inside a synagogue during the High Holy Days listening to a bunch of old bearded guys chanting in a language I didn't understand. As soon as I could possibly escape from religion and God, at thirteen, I did so—like a prisoner released from lock-up.

But for Sam, early on, religion was a powerful force to ponder and debate. Sam's mom is also not religious—she was born Christian—and when he was very young, Sam liked to tell people he was half-and-half, although technically, according to the orthodox and conservative Jews,

Sam would be officially Jewish only if his mom were Jewish. Reform Jews are not so selective—or at least, so I then thought. Originally, I had this idea that I would allow my son to choose his own religious direction by taking him periodically to different religious services. We've been to many churches and synagogues over the years. Sam says he is an atheist.

At one point, I decided to enroll him in an Episcopal Church Sunday school and a Reform Jewish Sunday school, simultaneously. He would attend alternate Sundays. Perhaps this was foolish and confusing, but Sam enjoyed the different experiences, until the rabbi from the Reform synagogue told me that Sam couldn't be educated as a Christian and a Jew at the same time, at least in her congregation. So I asked Sam if he wanted to make a choice. He did. I withdrew him from both Sunday schools and we have not returned to a church or synagogue in a regular or structured way since.

But as we traveled year after year, I came to believe that what we were doing in that truck when we went to the Grand Canyon and then the following year up the AlCan, ending at the peak of Exit Glacier, were in many ways religious experiences. In that truck, we were being monastic—we were contemplating the world in an incredibly intimate way by talking and relaxing into each other's silences. We were listening to the greatest music the world has ever known, from our point of view, music which demonstrably connected generations and cultures. Traveling, we were seeing the world, choosing to participate in a spontaneous and voluntary manner, while sharing the intimacy of a tiny comfortable chamber, not too different from a confession box, inside the truck. As Mr. Spock of *Star Trek* fame might put it, Sam and I, heading toward the Grand Canyon or Exit Glacier, and later venturing into China and Tibet and then visiting Auschwitz, were going through a mind meld, an extended religious experience no church, temple, cathedral, or museum could ever provide. The Creation Museum, however, provided an illuminating spotlight into a world we had automatically rejected.

WE ARE IN Noah's Cafe, sitting on high stools at a small high table, a very chic little place with lattes and cappuccinos and organic wraps featured on the menu, talking quietly, our heads together. Sam in Levi's and a wrinkled T-shirt displaying the periodic table is not so different in appearance from the other visitors to this brand new $27 million monument to the Book of Genesis called the Creation Museum. But the swarms of teens roaming this complex have T-shirts and badges displaying their faith. The biggest group, aside from Amish—there must be fifty kids, maybe more, banded together—display yellow-and-green Ts. The front side says "Covington California," while the back side reads "Runners on a Marathon Mission for God."

I am reading to Sam from the literature we've collected about this place, located in Petersburg, Kentucky, about fifty miles south of Cincinnati, and the few notes I have jotted down in my spiral reporters notebook.

"The state-of-the art 60,000-square-foot museum brings the pages of the Bible to life, casting its characters and animals in dynamic form and placing them in familiar settings. Adam and Eve live in the Garden of Eden. Children play and dinosaurs roam near Eden's rivers. The serpent coils cunningly in the Tree of Knowledge of Good and Evil." Behind us on the high stone wall snaking through the facility are advertisements for upcoming events, beginning with Answers Family Camp: Apologetics for the Whole Family, at the Higher Ground Conference Center, less than twenty minutes from the Museum.

There are six brass plaques embedded in the wall beginning at the entrance to the museum and spaced throughout the facility, organized according to the six Cs of History—Creation, Corruption, Catastrophe, Confusion, Christ, and Consummation.

Not surprisingly, the latter C is passed over quickly—in the blink of an eye. Signs everywhere: Prepare to Believe.

Bonnie—so says her "Volunteer" badge—approaches and introduces herself. "You are different from our regular visitors; I can tell by just looking at you," she said. "Why are you here?"

"We listened to a feature on NPR about this place. Sam was intrigued," I said, pointing at Sam. "So we came."

Bonnie nodded.

The Creation Museum took us by surprise—first because it is all so bizarre. I mean, putting prehistoric animals and humans together in the same place and time, for example, positioning Creationism with Darwinism, as if they are equally viable.

We had expected an onslaught of criticism of Darwinism and evolutionary theory, but the rhetoric turns out to be ingeniously subtle. Very little effort has been devoted to converting the unbelievers; the entire edifice concentrates on proving—indirectly, subtly—that the Creationists are right, and demonstrating how wrong the rest of us are. One of the first of 110 full-sized exhibits in the complex portrays two paleontologists on a dig working side-by-side at a site of dinosaur remains. On a video—one of fifty-two videos in the museum—above a life-sized diorama, both paleontologists address the audience, professing to be good friends and colleagues embarked on the same work with similar objectives, but different starting points.

The first paleontologist explains that he believes that the world started six thousand years ago when God created Adam and Eve. It is all presented in clear-cut fashion in the Book of Genesis. The dinosaurs, created on the sixth day, as described in Genesis, were on the ark with Noah, along with lions, giraffes, all living creatures. Later we learn that the transformations precipitated by the massive eruptions at Mt. St. Helens are a vivid demonstration of how the Grand Canyon came into being almost overnight during the flood that engulfed the Earth. All of his scientific exploration is anchored in that belief. "So, in fact," I tell Sam, "taking you to the Grand Canyon to show you evidence of the existence of God was the most legitimate religious experience I have ever provided for you."

The second archeologist, wielding shovel and brush, is basing his work on the fact that the world was created millions of years ago, as most scientists currently believe. The way in which the radically opposing viewpoints are presented—the spin—is quite ingenious and ever so daring.

"It's like George Bush," Sam says. "We're winning the war in Iraq!"

"It's a few levels more sophisticated than Bush," I say. "They're not saying that Creationism is right and the rest of the world is wrong. They're presenting the dialogue and the discourse so that both theories are on a level plane, that Creationism and Darwinism are comparable scientifically. That either theory could be right, depending on your starting point."

"If the Bible is your starting point," Sam says, "Everything follows and makes sense after that. Wendy has seen the light," he adds.

Sam is referring to the woman seeking meaning in life in the special-effects theatre in which the seats vibrate and the sky spits moisture to evoke a three dimensional image and reconstruction of the impact wrought by the flood. Wendy begins the show, appearing as a real person on stage and introducing the movie. "Prepare for some fun and prepare for some solid answers—some intriguing surprises—and PREPARE TO BELIEVE," she tells us.

The lights go down and Wendy sits on a stage in front of an artificial campfire emanating from a triple split screen. Then the celestial landscape suddenly appears as another voice, a haunting female voice, asks in the echoing stillness "Does anybody even know I am here? Is there any meaning? Did God create all of this or did we just invent God?"

Angelic voices echoing through the hall: *Hello—Hello—*

Suddenly a streak of white—like a falling star or a cosmic action—it comes and goes—lights up the sky in soft yellowish white—bright and inspiring. And then two men in white—angels—suddenly materialize out of the bright and inspiring light and into the atmosphere in a glorious crescendo of sweet soprano voices—and they hover above us until one says, "We are here, we are here—Gabe and I—for God actually. We didn't really invent God—God actually invented you."

It is a young man's voice—sincere—naive-enthusiastic—like a kid in college excited about life—"and everything else that matters," the angel continues, "the whole enchilada. The light, the dark, and the skies and the seas, the land and the plants and the birds and the bees—birds with wings and bugs that sing." They go on and on—and finally conclude with God as the ultimate educator. "He invented science," they declare definitively.

Now Wendy says something about science—"The voice of reason—scientific reason—how scientists helped kill polio and they invented cell phones—"

The angels smile scornfully: "She thinks that believing in God and creationism means that you have to reject science. She doesn't understand how God loves science. He tells people in his world to study creation; he wants us to know how he built everything—everything from neutrinos to eagles to the Milky Way—God made it all—protons, neutrons, photons"—again, they go on and on.

The film goes on for quite a while with amazing special effects. When the angels tell the story of the worldwide massive catastrophe—the flood and Noah's ark—the lights go on and off, thunder and lighting erupt, the chairs start to rumble and shake and the audience is sprayed with a light spritz of water.

Throughout the presentation Wendy is amazed and slowly she begins to see the reason and the plan of it all—a real transformation in belief. She is having a religious, rather than a religion, experience, we note, and she is amazed and moved. But the angels take it all in stride—they have witnessed and obviously precipitated such transformations before. "It is in the Bible," Wendy is told, "it is all in the Bible—when you start to look at the world through the perspective of the Bible—then all kinds of things start to make sense—like marine fossils found atop mountain ranges—those mountains were once covered in water—volcanic dust found in icecaps. Just think of all of the volcanic gas in the atmosphere after the flood—and the similarities in DNA found in the cells of every living thing. If you use the Bible as your starting point, Wendy, then everything makes sense."

Wendy is nodding now, gradually overcome with realization and clarity. "You see Wendy," the angels continue, "atheists and evolutionist can't see the hand of God because they really believe that there is no God. But you know better than that. Looking around you, God is clearly evident—just as clearly evident as there is a design for that chair you are sitting in. Your chair isn't just random pieces of wood that accidentally fell into place and randomly came together. Life even in its simplest form is way more complex than that. So doesn't it make sense that there should be a designer for life? And God is way more intelligent than that. He didn't just create the universe—he cares for it, sustains it and loves it. And God not only made all of this, but he also made you and He gives you freedom and purpose and life. This is an answer to the questions you have been asking Wendy—there is a God and you are way more than his creation. You must learn to know him in a personal way."

The movie continues—more religious philosophy, more scientific explanation, more common sense reasoning—but eventually, we tune out. And when it finally ends, we make our way into Noah's Café, amazed and impressed with the subtle and effective way in which propaganda and simplification blend with reality.

"What did you think of the movie," Bonnie asks us.

"Interesting," Sam says. Sam is being polite. Fortunately or unfortunately, Sam has not yet been tainted by the world to the extent that he knows how to lie. But I have.

"Fascinating," I say. "It really says a lot."

"It is so interesting that your son—that Sam"—she turns to look at him—"is curious about God and religion."

"He's been reading a lot about life's origins," I say.

"What are you reading Sam?"

"The Bible," Sam replies—and Bonnie smiles.

"Anything else"

"Richard Dawkins," naming the author *of The God Delusion*.

Bonnie blinks; her eyes cloud over. "What is your position on that?" Bonnie asks—meaning the existence of God.

"I think that that's a difficult question to answer," Sam replies.

Moshe Dann

AFTER THE WRITERS' CONFERENCE, fishing for halibut, and climbing Exit Glacier, which I will tell about in more detail a little later, we parked the Tundra on the ferry *Columbia,* which, after four days cruising the Inside Passage along the Alaskan Marine Highway, deposited us in Bellingham, Washington. We devoted a few days to touring Seattle, with special attention to the public library designed by Rem Koolhaas, and then meandered down the coast, through Oregon and California. It was beautiful—the Redwoods were especially breathtaking, unbelievably gigantic, unreal—cathedrals unto themselves. Along the way, we saw many signs comparing the redwoods with God and the divine, signs that Bonnie would have approved of: "These Trees," one sign said, "connect the earth to the Heavens." Another said, "Redwoods are God's anchor—a stabilizing force." Then there was: "Jesus Loves These Holy Trees" and "Redwoods are made in Christ's image."

From "Jesus Saves" to "The Buddha is Best" to "Stop Abortion Rights—Now!", wherever go you across the country, God and religion are inescapable. The more we traveled, the more we talked about the incredible and divisive impact religion has made in the United States and throughout the world—in Ireland where the Catholics battled the Protestants and in the Middle East, where Sunnis and Shiites, Israelis and Palestinians, seem concentrated on destroying each other. We were cognizant of the fact that the Israelis themselves were also at odds over religion—from atheism to ultra-orthodox—but could recognize the critical importance of having a country where, in fact, you were allowed to be at odds.

The Jews, before Israeli independence in 1948, were nomads. They went where they were permitted to live and where they were tolerated—sometimes for centuries and other times for only a few years, at best. They were not warriors—far from it. Many powerful men, with the force of great armies behind them, had tried for thousands of years to destroy them, but in some way, somehow, the Jews always managed to scratch out a living and survive.

Sam's Journal, 2008

In Israel, my dad and I made it a point to come out with some first-hand knowledge about the country's unique political situation. Though we had scheduled a private tour guide for walking tours of Jerusalem's Old City, Masada, the site of the Dead Sea Scrolls, and the Dead Sea itself, these historical escapades reflected very little on the present political environment that consumes Israel. We scheduled two more tours.

The first tour was hosted by a liberal activist organization known as "Ir Amim" and covered the Separation Wall, a gigantic array of concrete slabs stretching across Israel that divides communities occupied by Jews from those occupied by Arabs. The tour consisted of a long stop-and-go bus ride in which we viewed the wall surrounding Jerusalem from above, and stopped at several points along its perimeter. The guide focused on the hardships it created on the local communities—in one case, it had prevented an ambulance from delivering lifesaving medical treatment to a man because he lived in an Arab neighborhood outside the wall. She also commented on the present political division between the Israeli government and the autonomous governments of the Palestinian communities: for instance, nobody was monitoring or controlling what the Palestinian schools were teaching to their children. The guide acknowledged that she referred to newly built Palestinian neighborhoods as "communities," while calling new Israeli neighborhoods "settlements"—a word meant as a criticism, for they were inside occupied territory.

Seeking to look at both sides of the story, my father solicited a conservative Jewish tour guide named Moshe Dann, who categorically opposed any attempt to separate Israel into separate Jewish and Palestinian states. He had a characteristic way of pontificating; my first recollection of him was of my dad talking to him on the phone. My dad ended up spending fifteen or twenty minutes on a conversation that was supposed to resolve a quick, five-minute issue, during which time he seldom had the chance to open his mouth. Moshe also asked to call me Shmuel, my Hebrew name—par for the course, I figured, and so I obliged him.

Within the first ten seconds or so of our tour, however, Moshe revealed himself as a very knowledgeable, well-prepared contender in whatever battle there was to win the hearts and minds of foreign tourists. The instant I got into his car, he pointed out a collection of historical materials he had arranged for us on the back seat, which included a chronology of important moments in Israeli history, as well as a well-annotated copy of the Talmud. As we turned onto a major street, Moshe was able to point out a verse in the Talmud that he believed to be describing the exact same roadway. After we inadvertently made a remark indicating that we had taken a tour with Peace Now, he asked us for the name of the person who had recommended them to us, and assured us that today he would try to present to us a more balanced perspective.

The first stop on our tour was Gush Etzion, a bloc of Jewish villages built in the disputed West Bank that had been destroyed by Arabs in the 1948 Arab-Israeli War. Parts of the settlement have been rebuilt. One of them now houses an auditorium, in which Moshe showed us a video on the history of Gush Etzion. It depicted a vibrant community filled with motivated people, struggling to build a community against the forces of the elements, nobly fighting against Arabs who would eventually torch their buildings and then leave the land barren and desolate. This was a recurring theme throughout Moshe's tour—most of Israel consists of deserted land owned by nobody, "state land" as he called it, and whereas ideological Israelis want to expand into these untouched horizons, Palestinians seem to have little drive to make use of it. But they don't want to give up the land; they would rather leave it barren.

As the highlight of our trip, Moshe had ambitiously arranged to drive us to Hebron—the largest city in the occupied West Bank, home to more than 160,000 Palestinians and fewer than 600 Israelis. Moshe took us straight into the heart of this besieged Jewish section, which is crammed with temples, historic sites, and single-story dwellings packed atop one another. Some of the towers atop these residential buildings unmistakably sprout machine gun nests, which are also to be found at street corners and various other strategic locations. Moshe showed us a neighborhood of abandoned buildings, from which Jews had been apparently evicted according to some arrangement with the Israeli government and the Palestinians. A sign on one of the buildings reads, in large, capital letters: "These buildings were constructed on land purchased by the Hebron Jewish community in 1807. This land was stolen by Arabs following the murder of 67 Hebron Jews in 1929. We demand justice! Return our property to us! The Jewish community of Hebron."

Moshe also showed us the Peace House, a home owned by a Jewish couple located at the very border between Arab and Jewish neighborhoods. A patrol of Israeli soldiers was stationed outside the house at all times. The wife recounted a story to us in which a crowd of eighty Arabs had swarmed their house. The troops were forbidden from firing their weapons, even into the air. Her husband had been struggling to keep the Arabs at bay with his martial arts skills. But the Arabs finally dispersed when she began beating them over their heads with her mop.

Radio Shack

MY MOTHER, Mollie Gutkind, and the woman in Hebron with the mop, seem to be considerably more effective at winning battles than Jewish men.

Not too long ago, I took my mother to a nearby Radio Shack so that she could purchase a new cell phone and choose a new service provider. While the transaction was still in process—we were transferring from her current service provider to a competitor—my mother was at the cash register purchasing, separately, for cash, a 9-volt battery for her smoke alarm. I wasn't paying a lot of attention, nor was Sam, who was occupied with his own battery needs. The store was bustling with browsing customers, like Sam, examining gadgets, reading product descriptions, and asking questions. My thoughts were drifting, wondering why Sam has had such a long and ongoing fascination with batteries and his continuous comparison and dialogue about disposables vs. rechargeables when, suddenly, I heard my mother's voice, and when I looked, she was shaking her finger and yelling, "You stole from me! I want my money back!"

Her anger and her finger were directed at the Radio Shack sales clerk, a plump, baby-faced young man in his early twenties named Caleb, who was standing behind the cash register holding a five-dollar bill in his hand. Caleb was new on the job—still in training, judging by the slow and methodical way in which he had handled the cell phone transaction. Now at the cash register, he seemed taken aback by my mother's outburst. "This is the bill that you gave me," he said, waving the greenback like a handkerchief, "and I gave you ninety eight cents change," he pointed to the money on the counter. The battery was $4.02.

"But I gave you a ten-dollar bill," my mother said. "And that five dollars is what you owe me—not what I gave you. You can keep this change." She pushed the coins toward him across the counter. "But I want the cash."

My mother is 89 years old—and a miracle, some might say. She's healthy, articulate, and although hard of hearing and somewhat forgetful, basically self-sufficient. She lives in our family home, alone—which was actually her father's house, and then, when my grandfather died, the house she shared with my dad—and, as long as the weather is mild, she walks twice a week to the supermarket a few blocks away and carries her groceries, including cans and bottles, back home. She doesn't drive, never has, but she's lucky enough to have a few remaining friends her age who are still driving. They'll take her to restaurants for those late-afternoon early bird specials once or twice a week, and she'll usually take leftovers home so that she has lunch or dinner the following day. She'll also use public transportation for her weekly visit to the beauty shop or to one of her numerous doctors' appointments.

Sometimes she gets scared, though. Recently, there was a series of incidents in which she thought she couldn't breathe—until the paramedics wanted to take her to the Emergency Room, at which point she miraculously, in the blink of an eye, recovered. In response to that incident, I convinced her to undergo an intensive examination—every conceivable test Medicare would pay for. She passed with flying colors and has not experienced any panic attacks since—unless you want to count this incident at Radio Shack. Actually, Caleb, facing this old blue-haired lady with the wagging finger demanding money and yelling "I've been cheated!" so that everyone in the store could hear her and look at him with suspicion for trying to cheat a defenseless old lady, may have been experiencing his own panic attack.

"You gave me five dollars," he said again, talking slowly to accentuate his patience and professionalism. "We only have one ten dollar bill in the register," he pointed down at his open cash drawer, "and that has been there all day."

But my mother, unimpressed by his polite approach, was still yelling and wagging her finger: "I don't care what you have in the cash register—I know how much money I had in my wallet—This is something I always know," she stressed, "and how much I gave you; I won't be cheated or taken advantage of."

By this time, I was back at the scene of the crime at the cash register. I took the receipt from the sales clerk's hand; he had been about to put the receipt in the bag with the battery, as was his routine. "It says here," I said to my mother, "that you gave him five dollars. It is clearly marked. He gave you ninety eight cents change."

"I don't care what it says," my mother told me, "I know how much money I had in my wallet—there was a ten dollar bill and eight ones—and now," she opened the flap of her wallet and motioned for me to look inside, "the ten is gone because that is what I gave him. The eight ones are still here."

I nodded and hesitated, taking stock. Just a few minutes ago, she was whispering in a very conspiratorial tone to Caleb about how much she hates cell phones and doesn't really want one because it is such a waste of money since she never uses it, and she is only getting it for emergency purposes because, basically, her children insisted that she have one, despite the cost, especially if you consider her previous cell phone, which didn't work too well inside her house—she had to go out onto the front porch in order to take advantage of the free minutes, very inconvenient, especially in the middle of the winter—and so on.

"The receipt says," I repeated, "that you only gave him a five." I tapped my finger on the item marked on the smooth while strip of paper, but she refused to even look.

"Anybody can say what they want on a receipt." She looked at Caleb. "I wasn't born yesterday," she said.

By this time, there were a number of customers waiting in line behind her to pay for purchases and those around the store, browsing, were all turned in our direction, watching the action. There was a woman waiting in the line who was being helped by the other clerk, an older man, to whom she said, motioning to my mother, "Why don't you check your receipts at the end of the day, and then you will know the truth? You can call her if the register is five dollars over and you can return the money."

"Let them check their receipts at the end of the day and see if the register is five dollars over," I said to my mother. "It's only five dollars, and you'll have it back tomorrow or tonight if you're right—you don't need it now."

"Five dollars may not be important to you—you're a big shot—but to me, it's a lot of money." Her hand was in the air, her finger still wagging. My mother's face is relatively youthful; you'd never guess she was eighty-nine. But you can read her age in her hands, blemished with liver marks and scarred with gnarled blue veins. "Let them give me the five dollars they owe me and then they can check their register at the end of the day and if it's five dollars short, they can call me and tell me."

"Would you give it back if it was?" Caleb said to my mother.

"I'll have to think about it," she replied.

"Really," I said to her, not so much embarrassed as impatient, "it's only five dollars."

"Five dollars may not mean anything to you, but that's a lot of money for me; I can't afford to lose it."

"But that's not true," I said.

"What?" she asked, rather sharply. "You think you know how much money I have? Who are you—my attorney?"

I hesitated, not knowing how to answer. I did, in fact, have a pretty good idea how much money my mother had, since I have had conversations with my brother, who is the executor of our mother's will. "And do you know, Mr. Big Shot," she continued, "how much the five dollars you want me to give away means to me?"

I looked at my mother and didn't reply. To her the five dollars meant more than money. I should have realized this, but the drama of the moment caught me off guard. To my mom, whose parents came from Russia at the turn of the century and were nearly annihilated by everyone—neighbors, Marxist revolutionaries, the Russian Guard—money represents a lifetime of denial and hard work and the survival of her culture, since, like most Jews down through the ages, she has no real nationality or homeland that matters anymore.

My father's parents also made it to America from Poland and Germany before the Nazis began their systematic slaughter, but most members of the Gutkind family did not—or at least that's what we thought for many years.

WHEN MY FATHER retired in the 1980s, he frequently visited the business branch of the Carnegie Library in downtown Pittsburgh, leafing through available telephone books from different parts of the world, seeking people with our last name—or a close derivative. "Gutkind" was in parentheses after *Goodchild, Sam*, in the Melbourne, Australia phonebook, so my father wrote a letter. Three weeks later the phone rang and the long lost familial connection was remade. Sam Goodchild, it turned out, was an Australian millionaire now; how he had made his fortune, though, was a mystery he declined to discuss. My father insisted that "Uncle" Sam's wealth emanated from the black market, an elusive term, somehow related to drug-trafficking, money laundering, and illegal weapons, endeavors linked to the contacts he had made during the war when he was a fugitive, having fought his way out of the Warsaw ghetto in 1938 and disappeared through the rest of the war in the French countryside. But this was unsubstantiated, romanticized theory.

Few other Gutkinds, including my dad, unfortunately, had acquired the knack for coming up with money, mysterious and otherwise—or so we thought then. Isadore, my father's father, a tailor, was especially strapped for cash. He was a pious orthodox Jew who, seemingly, devoted every available moment to his synagogue and to philosophical discussions, examinations, and explanations of the Talmud and Torah. There were always visitors in heavy black coats and fur hats, drinking hot tea out of clear water-glasses in Isadore's living room or on his rooftop porch chatting in Yiddish. But when Isadore died in the late 1960s, a key was found in the old, battered black prayer book he always carried around with him. The prayer book had been Isadore's most treasured possession, and was invariably by his side or on his lap, a hand resting on its cover. And no wonder.

The key was to a safety deposit box no one knew he had, filled with cash, stocks, and bonds. No one in the family now remembers or was willing to discuss how much money Isadore had amassed, but the amount was clearly substantial and puzzling—especially considering that Isadore lived quite modestly in Squirrel Hill, a Jewish ghetto, in a walk-up apartment on the second level of a kosher delicatessen and fish market. He and his second wife, Molly, shared a two-bedroom apartment with a family of four, named Levy.

As a kid, I always tried to pee in our own bathroom at home before our family visits to Isadore and Molly, because to get to their bathroom you had to walk up the stairs and into Mr. and Mrs. Levy's part of the apartment and down a hallway, passing their living room and bedroom. I always felt like an enemy invader—a spy. During most days, Mrs. Levy often had a nightgown on and Mr. Levy seemed to spend a lot of his time in bed. In the summers when we visited, especially in the evenings when it was dark, I'd often sneak out into the small backyard and pee behind the house, so I didn't have to go up into the Levy's territory.

Why my grandfather chose to live so frugally with all of his secret money, the family had no clue. Why he felt the need to have such substantial hidden assets, or how he had accumulated his wealth in the first place (he evidently had a close relationship with a stockbroker with whom he communicated buy-sell instructions once or twice a week), is another question we could not answer, unless, of course, you want to think about the history of the Jewish people and his decimated extended family. Money could buy escape and survival—secret money no one could easily confiscate. As a tailor, Isadore, along with Molly, a seamstress, generated a modest income along with their social security checks. My father supplemented their income, a fact that annoyed my father to no end when he learned of Isadore's stash. "He could have also received more money from Social Security," my father told me later, "I found a way—a loophole. But he kept saying, 'No, I don't want to cheat the government.'"

Now, as I reflect back, it wasn't so much that Isadore didn't want to cheat the government; he didn't want to attract attention. I didn't understand this philosophy then. It seemed absurd because I was young and felt free—I was imprisoned by my father's stern hand and our family and religious values, however—but certainly not by this country, the home of the brave and the land of the free. At the time, I saw no reason to think otherwise or to sympathize with my grandfather. That was before visiting Auschwitz and Theresienstadt.

Rose

IN 2008, the same year we visited Israel, Sam and I went to Terezin in the Czech Republic, about an hour's bus ride outside Prague. I had actually never heard of Terezin. I was invited to Prague to conduct a two-week workshop for an American university with a summer program there. I came across Terezin in a tour book. The Germans had renamed the town Theresienstadt, but after the war the Czechs took back the original name. Initially, it didn't interest me because I had already decided that since we were going to be in the Czech Republic we would take a side trip to Auschwitz-Birkenau in Poland, an eight-hour train ride from Prague. No need to see a minor detention camp when you can experience the mother of all concentration camps, I thought.

Circumstances changed when I arrived in Prague. We took a tour of the old Jewish Quarter there, destroyed by the Nazis during the war but recently having undergone somewhat of a renaissance, as has Prague itself. Jewish population before the war was 50,000 in Prague, with nearly 125,000 throughout the rest of the country, although today there are fewer than 3,000 Jews remaining nationwide.

The vast majority of Czech Jews were taken to Theresienstadt. Nearly 140,000 people were deported there in all, including gypsies and patients from mental hospitals, 33,000 of whom died, with most of the rest taken to extermination camps like Auschwitz and murdered. Fewer than 200 children and 1,700 adults had survived when the camp was liberated in 1945, according to Rose, our guide.

You didn't have to tell me that Rose was one of those Theresienstadt survivors; the pain and misery of her past was written on her face.

Cheeks wrinkled like prunes—eyes too bright, like those of a deer caught in the headlights of an oncoming train, the Nazi horde. Her voice was flat, void of timbre and definition, transmitting a single, breathless, shallow dimension of sound. I can't imagine how or why she had become a tour guide. Neither could she, it seemed, as she searched our faces for recognition and asked, every time she led us from one spot to another, "Yes?"

Perhaps she was just seeking moral support from us, for it seemed as if we had come upon Rose in the midst of a turf battle she was destined to lose. The tour began in the Gothic Old-New (Or "Alt-Neu") Synagogue, Europe's oldest active synagogue, completed in 1270. Those of us in front of the group, closest to Rose, could hear the essence of her explanation regarding why the synagogue was both old and new. According to Yiddish documents, the synagogue was originally called the Great Synagogue and later, when newer synagogues were built around the city, it became known as the Old-New Synagogue. More pious Jews tell a different story. They say that the synagogue was built from stones from the Temple in Jerusalem "on condition" that the stones would be returned after the reconstruction of the Temple. Surely we weren't supposed to believe that the stones were actually carried from Jerusalem. That would have been quite a hike—or a boat ride. But as I said, hardly anyone in our group, except for me and Sam and a woman I will call Beth, could hear and understand what Rose was saying.

Inexplicably, Klara, a large Czech woman with a booming voice and an overcoming presence, had launched her tour of the Jewish quarter at the same time. So throughout the tour, wherever Rose went, Klara was not far behind or, for that matter, wherever Klara was, Rose led us in the same general direction. So Rose, whose voice was thin and brittle as crystal, was constantly drowned out by Klara's booming drumbeat. Klara was articulate; she pontificated and she projected; from time to time we were tempted to slip away from Rose's group and blend into Klara's, but we realized that that would be rude and devastating to Rose, who had clearly been the target of enough rude and destructive behavior in her lifetime. So I stuck with Rose, as did Sam—and Beth.

Beth, in her late 50s, was a therapist from California who had registered for the workshop I was teaching, but she was actually in Prague to see her relatives and reconnect with her past. It occurred to me almost immediately that Beth could have been Rose's daughter. They resembled one another in some ways—short and slight, pale complexion, short hair and tiny hands. But the similarities that really registered with me were rather subtle. Rose's eyes mirrored Beth's. There was something frantic about what she was seeing from those eyes, a lack of control, an edge of desperation. Her voice was similarly frail like Rose's—even shallower and less robust—hard to imagine. Beth had been to Theresienstadt twice in the two weeks she had been in Prague, but was now going back a third time, for she had been able, through research online, to locate the barracks in which her great aunt had lived.

Beth hadn't known her aunt, obviously; she had died in Theresienstadt. Her father, Beth said, who had left Prague a few months before the Nazi occupation, had never gotten over his guilt for not dying with his sister or not rescuing her. Before the war, his sister was the apple of the family's eye—the chosen child—and her father's parents had urged her father to do whatever was necessary to rescue her. He failed—and he was, throughout the rest of his life, haunted by the notion that he had not fulfilled his mission as a good son. The family was similarly haunted by stories of this sister, the perfect child. Beth and her two sisters lived in the shadow of the death of her aunt. Beth had a vast catalogue of photographs passed on to her, documenting her father's life in Prague before the war—images he had escaped with—combined with more photographs of the relatives who had remained and survived in the Czech Republic, in and around Prague.

This I learned as Rose led us behind the Old-New Synagogue, followed closely by Klara's group, and into the old Jewish cemetery, where Beth thought that some of her relatives may have been buried, although finding such a grave would occur only by chance since, according to Rose and Klara, the Jews in this cemetery, space severely limited by the walls of the ghetto, were buried in layers, one on top of another, with fifty-five centimeters of earth, or, as Rose put it, "fifty-five centimeters of holy air," between the bodies. So even if Beth had found the gravestone of one of her relatives, she would have no idea how many layers down the remains were buried. Most of Prague had survived the war intact, which was one of the reasons for Prague's renaissance today, so there was the possibility that the cemetery had not been vandalized and her relatives' remains were close. The Czech people had assumed ownership of the Jewish assets and property, however. The Jews, after all, were in Theresienstadt—or Auschwitz.

The distinction between death in a detention camp and death in a concentration camp is in some ways nebulous. In Auschwitz-Birkenau, people were selected upon arrival for extermination—mostly children, women, and old people—those most likely to be less productive from a manual-labor point of view. They went directly to the gas chambers. The more healthy Auschwitz internees worked at a number of different jobs until they became too weak or sick to work, and then they were killed. The internees at Theresienstadt were in limbo. Crammed like sardines in newly constructed barracks or existing makeshift buildings, they too worked night and day until they died—in a survival-of-the-fittest situation. When the camp became bursting with humanity, the Germans would simply select the weakest or the most troublesome for transfer to Auschwitz, where they were gassed and then cremated.

As in Auschwitz, those who died at Theresienstadt were also cremated, and when we visited, Sam and I walked through the crematorium where the people who died there were disposed of. It was all very quiet and subdued, people coming and going cautiously, with trepidation, almost as if they were fearful of waking the dead until, suddenly, a man, middle aged, dropped down on his knees, opened up his backpack, took out a red rose with a long stem, and placed it on top of the ovens. They had big wide doors, like pizza ovens. The man took out two candles and lit them, then lowered his head and began to pray. I tapped him on the shoulder as we walked by to show my support, and he looked up to stare at me. No one else seemed to pay any attention. You feel self-conscious there in that furnace of evil and doom. You can't help thinking, "How did I live, why did I live, when everyone else, all these many thousands of Jews, died?

Aunt Hattie

JACK GUTKIND, my father, was born in the Lawrenceville section of Pittsburgh. At that time, his father, Isadore, owned a neighborhood dry goods store. My father's mother, Leah, my namesake, got sick before his tenth birthday, so my father was frequently kept home from school to help operate the store, the only employee. Neither the store nor the quarters above where they lived at the time were equipped with electricity. There were gas mantels for light and a pot-bellied stove for heat in the kitchen. Firing up the boiler was permitted only on days they took baths.

Eventually, the family moved to Queens, where Leah's health became more critical. On the day she signed my father's registration for high school, Hebrew Polytechnic, she was sitting up in a wheelchair for the first time in months. When my father returned after school, his mother was dead.

It was February 1st, 1929, a Friday, and she was buried on a Sunday. As was the custom, most orthodox Jews did not go to a funeral home, and they did not bury their dead during the Sabbath. So, after sundown on Saturday, Leah's body was transported home from the hospital. "She was laid out in the living room with candles at her head—no coffin," my father once wrote in a letter to me. "In the morning, a wooden casket was brought in, covered with a black velvet shawl with a Star of David on it. I can't express my feelings of what that did to me, my mother dead in the living room all night long. Orthodox Jews in heavy black clothing said prayers through the following night. She was buried at Beth David cemetery, Long Island, New York, on Sunday."

Some months after his mother's death, after the family had once again relocated in Pittsburgh, my father came home from school. Isadore was absent, but my father was directed by a cousin to the home of another relative. A wedding had just taken place, and my father arrived in the middle of a celebratory dinner. He was ushered into the room and seated across from a woman he had neither seen nor met before. This was Isadore's new wife—my father's new mother—the seamstress and the future heiress of my grandfather's fortune, Molly.

Soon after, my father left home and restarted life alone. He worked in a fruit store, as a Western Union boy delivering telegrams, sold newspapers and peanuts and football souvenirs, which he designed and made himself, with the appropriate school colors. After graduating high school, he worked in a machine shop and as a draftsman. But this was in the height of the Depression and the company soon went bankrupt. For a while, he sold razor blades. Then he began reconditioning used automobile spark plugs, purchased for a penny apiece. My father sanded and repainted them, set the gaps, had special boxes made which said, "Jack's Spark Plugs, Guaranteed Reconditioned," then resold them back to the garages for retail sale to customers. This sounded incredibly boring and tedious to me—and these days much more costly than simply buying new spark plugs, but since my father could not get a job, like nearly half of the working force in the nation in 1936, time and initiative were his greatest assets.

Before and after World War II, my father, a self-described "shoe dog," worked in shoe stores all around the Western Pennsylvania–West Virginia corridor, a 150-mile radius of Pittsburgh. I had also worked in the shoe store, a children's shoe store primarily, specializing in orthopedic footwear, which he opened in the late 1950s—called Tryson's (pronounced "Tri-sons"), for his three sons. He used "Tryson" instead of "Tri-son" because he thought it looked better with a Y. Most people thought Tryson was his last name; they didn't get the three sons significance.

In retrospect, I like to think of my father as a pioneer of consumer branding—first with his spark plugs and then later in his little shoe store in the Pittsburgh suburbs, where he began buying shoes from small, unknown companies, mostly in eastern Pennsylvania, Amish country, settled for centuries by German leather craftsmen—high in quality but considerably less expensive than the well-known brands like Poll Parrot and Stride Rite. Back in the corner of the stockroom was a tiny workbench with knives, razor blades, and pliers to remove the original heel pads with the brand name of the shoes emblazoned on them, a ballpoint pen to trace the original heel pad onto a sheet of leather he purchased in bulk, and a jar of petroleum-based rubber cement. There, a worker would rip the heel pads out of the original off-branded shoes, trace, cut out and glue in a replacement heel pad with my father's brand, Tryson's. My father would make certain that the heel pad was of higher quality than the original—leather verses some sort of paper or composition material—and then he'd increase the retail price of the shoe by a dollar or two. This was branding, long before Apple and Starbucks and MacDonald's became household names.

It has taken me a while to recognize the brilliance of my father's vision, probably because the person he corralled into ripping out the original shoe labels and gluing in the Tryson's branded ones was his first-born son, me, for eight hours a day, every Saturday and also a couple days every week after school. My head still aches with the memory of the fumes from the petroleum-based rubber cement. Usually, I was permitted to play the radio back in that lonely cubbyhole where I worked, as long as it wasn't too loud.

MY FATHER WAS THE youngest of three children. Ethel, a sister who lived in Queens, married to Leon, a stockbroker, was the middle child. Leon seemed considerably older than Ethel and suffered from a heart condition. As a boy, I only met Leon a few times. He was balding, with a band of white hair surrounding his pink shiny dome, a long pale nose, shaped with a dip like a ski lift. He seemed rather stuffy; didn't have a lot to say about most anything that did not relate to financial markets. Family legend was that he was very wealthy—how could he not be, people asked—a New York stockbroker? But their apartment in Queens was quite modest, as was the apartment Ethel and their son Larry moved to in Pittsburgh after Leon died—two bedrooms, a living room, and a dining area. But Ethel was secretive about her money, dropping hints that she knew the stock market up and down just like Isadore and Leon; she lived on her dividends, and her trading opportunities and acumen were making her a fortune, or so my father and mother said.

Hattie, married to Lou, who owned a hardware store, was the eldest. Uncle Lou was someone I was close to when I was a kid, a real father figure, much more sensitive and loving at times than my own dad; Lou took me to see all of the TV and movie-star cowboys who made appearances in town at the time: Hopalong Cassidy, Roy Rogers and Dale Evans, and Gene Autry. I met them all, personally, shook their hands and patted their horses' behinds, courtesy of Lou, who purchased tickets and talked his way backstage. These events were highlights of my childhood. But something happened—some secret conflict—between my parents and Hattie, and they did not talk for many years. The family, once big and boisterous, suddenly shrunk. Lou was banned (by Hattie) from seeing me or taking me to shake hands with cowboys. Years later, after Lou had died, my parents and Hattie began to see each other again, I am not exactly sure of the how or why, but by then I was pretty much out of touch with the family myself and was completely estranged from Hattie.

The way Hattie cut me off from Lou really hurt me, so I decided not to talk with her. This seems rather arbitrary and irrational now—and I wish I could take it back—for the isolation and separation never ended. Years later, I would see Hattie on the street in Squirrel Hill sometimes, only a few blocks from Isadore's walk-up. Usually, she'd be at the corner of Forbes and Murray Avenues near the Jewish Community Center, where senior citizens could pass the time of day and receive a free lunch. The JCC was next door to Sam's school.

I usually avoided direct contact with Hattie when I saw her, although once I walked right by her, within arm's reach, with Sam, then a baby in his backpack on my shoulders, and I said, "Hello," just as I might have greeted any stranger on the street. This was in the mid-1990s. Ethel was dead and Larry had left town. Hattie had gained a lot of weight by then and was having trouble walking—she used a walker—and she had evidently given up bathing and brushing her teeth, which were caked a filthy yellow color when she smiled, as I greeted her. I'm positive she didn't know me—and I did not tell her who I was—but that was the closest she ever came to meeting Sam, since she had exiled Lou—and the cowboys—from me so many years before.

But the day before she died, Hattie suddenly, out of the blue, telephoned me. Even after all of those years, I recognized her voice immediately. "Hello, Lee," she said in her singsong manner. Though she had lived most of her adult life in Pittsburgh, Hattie was born and raised in New York and you could still hear the faint echoes of Brooklyn in her pronunciation of "R" words, as in New *Yawk* and *Dawling*, which is what she called me that day, "Lee, *Dawling*, I am returning your phone call."

I said that I hadn't called her—she was mistaken, it must be another Lee; maybe it was Lou, not Lee, I joked, checking in from the Great Beyond. She said that she was certain that she had heard my message on her answering machine correctly, *Dawling, it was you*, and that she recognized my voice and in any case, she went on, even if I didn't call her, I should have been calling her for many years and bringing Sam over to her house to meet her. I don't recall how the conversation progressed from that point, although she said that she had been hearing my voice quite regularly over those past few weeks, *You were calling to me, Lee, Dawling, and I was trying to answer*, which we both agreed was rather odd. As clearly as I can remember, that's how our conversation ended. I got a phone call the very next morning from my father saying that Hattie was dead. She died only a few hours after we talked.

I've always wondered why Hattie had called me—if she had really heard my voice, or if I had really telephoned (maybe I did and can't remember or won't admit it)—and if, in fact, as I go back over it in my mind, repeatedly mulling the situation, I should have been more responsive once the contact was made, after maybe two decades of silence. I could have come over and visited her or promised that I would soon bring Sam to meet her. Maybe I would be a rich man today if I would have been a bit more compassionate and forgiving when I heard Hattie's voice. I don't know. Maybe she was calling me in a subtle silent expression—an open door to her assets and my inheritance.

My father had had a key to Hattie's apartment for years, although he had never used it or been invited inside. Even when he would drive over to pick her up to take her somewhere—supermarket, synagogue, etc.—he had not been allowed in. No one in the family as far as I know had been permitted to enter Hattie's apartment since the day Uncle Lou had died. My father let himself into the apartment only after Hattie was pronounced dead the following morning and after we had talked. Hattie died in her sleep.

The apartment was very dark, my father reported, and there were newspapers in stacks along the wall or stuffed into corners, barricading doors, newsprint everywhere. Hattie evidently had not thrown out a paper for a decade, judging by the dates. And there were brown paper shopping bags from supermarkets half-empty with food that Hattie had purchased, brought home, but forgotten to put in cupboards—or refrigerate, now rotting—lining the apartment entryway, dumped in the kitchen. Scattered about the entire apartment were also piles of those sugar packets, and the tiny jelly containers and butter patties you get free at restaurants—a maze of shit, according to my father, who methodically worked his way through the hallways, living room and kitchen and into the bedroom.

Here, Hattie's clothes were strewn about everywhere, on the floor, hanging on lamps, under the bed—reeking of food, perspiration and filth—but Lou's clothes had all been neatly preserved in the closets, laundered, folded, pressed, and cleaned since, conceivably, 1977, when he died. I don't know how long it took for my father to notice the bulges in the pockets of Lou's shirts and jackets—or what he might have said (or yelled!) when he first began to investigate and reach inside. But what he found was amazing: Those pockets were filled with cash and stock certificates and savings account passbooks. Money! The more my father—my mother joined him—rooted about in the filth and mess, the more wealth they discovered. It actually took a few years to collect and account for all of Hattie's assets—for stocks and bonds and CDs kept turning up in safety deposit boxes or coming due and suddenly appearing in the mail—a small fortune, my father said.

This was actually how I knew, more or less, how much money my mother had stashed away in the bank. It is ironic but true, but until Hattie died and her assets were accounted for, my parents had very little. Mostly they were living on Social Security. My father, as her nearest blood relative, got half the Hattie money, and cousin Larry inherited the other half.

MY MOTHER'S APPRECIATION of money and her understanding of its value in different contexts are kind of limited and unimaginative. Take the cell phone we got for her—her first cell. She was not unaware of having to pay fifty dollars per month for two years for the baseline call package. She considered that the cost of doing business, the fee for living in America in a free society—like paying real estate taxes. What delighted her were the free weekend minutes she got with the deal—anytime after nine o'clock in the evening on Friday all the way through Sunday midnight. She was excited about the prospect of telephoning friends and relatives wintering in Florida or my brother who lives in Philadelphia and talking endlessly, long distance, without having to pay a dime. This turned her on. Never mind the fact that she did not use the minutes for which she was paying—this would be a waste. She was saving those minutes for emergencies. When I was growing up, she was always buying me super-nice dress clothes, sale items, to wear on special occasions, like weddings or bar mitzvahs, but whenever I wanted to wear the clothes to go to parties or other more ordinary events, she wouldn't permit it. "Why not?" I would ask. "I'm growing out of these clothes and I'll never be able to benefit from having them."

"Because," she would reply, "we are saving them 'for good.'"

Good, I guess, meant some incredibly fancy or important event that I/we/the family might be invited to, like the inauguration of the president of the United States or my induction into the Baseball Hall of Fame in Cooperstown. We had to have such clothes "for good" just in case. This phone plan represented a similar situation. You took advantage of the free minutes and saved the minutes for which you paid "for good," meaning for emergencies, for things that happen when you least expect them, such as when you get a phone call from Publisher's Clearing House, making certain you are home before they deliver your winning check for $10 million. Saving for good also meant saving for survival. Many Jews of my parents' generation still believed that Christian America would turn against them. Some Jews believe it now.

But the entire cell phone adventure turned sour because, for some reason, the signal of the service provider (Verizon) we had selected for my mother could not penetrate the thick walls of her old house. I had a different provider, and my cell phone worked perfectly fine in the house, as did Sam's—still another service provider. In her house, she still held on to her landline, but losing the free minutes was driving her crazy, and she complained bitterly and frequently.

"So let's dump Verizon and get something else," I told her repeatedly, but my mother refused because of the $125 cancellation fee. "It will cost me money!"

"But you can't use the phone. You're wasting $50 a month."

"I am not going to pay $125 for no reason and not get anything back from it—that's not fair. I won't do it—I can't afford it."

Which is what she had insisted at Radio Shack—but I knew she had half of Hattie's money, which was not unsubstantial. But the fact that she had a healthy bank account did not deter my mother from the battle for the five dollars from Caleb for one instant. She continued to shake her fist and yell and scream. And then, when Caleb put the five dollars down on the counter to turn to his manager for help, my mother picked it up and put it in her wallet; and despite Caleb's protests, she would not give it back. "This belongs to me," she insisted. And from that moment, at least—it did.

In Auschwitz there's an entire room filled with the shoes of those who perished there, plus rooms or room-sized display cases crammed with confiscated pots and pans, combs and brushes, blankets and bedding, clothes, suitcases—and more—all discovered by the Russians who liberated the camp in 1945. One can only imagine, considering the 1.5 million people who died there, the inestimable mountain of confiscated possessions that the Nazis took to distribute to their soldiers or families in the Homeland—or to hoard, saving perhaps, for their own "good." There's even a display case/room with the hair severed from their victims—as well as the blankets into which the hair was fused. Our tour guide that day, Daria, whose presentation was dramatic and articulate, led us through this series of rooms in absolute silence. The shoes, along with the other confiscated possessions, said it all. Later, at Yad Veshem in Israel, we saw the movies of the assassination squads we had first seen in the Holocaust Museum in Washington in even more intense detail—and from an overwhelming multitude of angles and monitors. There were more stacks of looted personal items, including shoes.

Shoes are the most personal of all possessions, I think. You can wash clothes, dry-clean sweaters, and then lend them out to friends and family—and wear them, washed or unwashed, when they are returned. But people mark their shoes with the shape of their feet, which is as unique to an individual as are his fingerprints. Not to mention the odor, moisture, one of a kind to a person's feet. The markings on the inside and outside, the ways in which the owners of these shoes broke them in, the intimate creases in the leather, the telltale scuffs that make the shoes part of the person, are still there in Auschwitz from three quarters of a century ago. In this way, the people who wore the shoes will never entirely die.

Because of my father, the images of these shoes are especially significant to me—there's also a room crammed with children's shoes—because shoes have been a part of my life as far back as I can remember. I have always felt that my father, an angry and distant person, made his intimate connection with the world through feet. I cannot remember my father in our home ever kissing or touching with tenderness; his attempts at intimacy were awkward, but he caressed his customer's feet—which made him a natural as a "shoe dog"—nomenclature for the close cadre of shoe merchants he networked with. People will sometimes laugh when I tell them my dad was a "shoe dog," but he was fond of the phrase. "It's my lifeline," he said. "It's how I make my money."

"Money's not everything," I once told him, when I was a lot younger and more idealistic.

"If you're Jewish," he told me, somewhat angrily, "it sometimes almost is."

Getting Lost and Losing It

AFTER ZIGZAGGING through the redwoods from Washington and Oregon and following the California coastline down to Los Angeles, we turned east and worked our way up into the San Juan Mountains in southwestern Colorado, which cover about an eighth of the entire state. The five-hundred-mile Colorado Trail, part of which Sam and I would later hike in 2006, snakes through the San Juans, with peaks among the highest and most rugged in North America, rising above fourteen thousand feet. The area was actually developed first for gold and silver mining and many of the major towns, now famous ski resorts, were once bustling mining camps, like Telluride, Lake City, Silverton, and Ouray.

What's eerie and wonderful about Ouray is the contrast of knowing that you are sitting six thousand feet high, far above almost everywhere. Yet, everywhere you look, the mountains surround you, ringing the town in every direction, as if you are in a valley. The mountains are literally rings. The burnished brown layers of rock, dotted with trees, are clearly defined in a jagged circle. A half-dozen waterfalls—icy flowing white lines—are etched into the mountains.

A few days ago, while on our way to Silverton, Jill Patterson, the friend we were visiting, navigated her Jeep along the twisting, climbing, switchback while pointing out the places where people had died or disappeared on this forty-mile stretch of highway which, according to the AAA, is the most harrowing stretch of road in America. "There's the monument," said Jill, pointing to a modest stone marker with a cross and a plaque at the opposite end of an avalanche tunnel. "A monument," she added, "to miscalculation and overconfidence."

More people die in avalanches on this stretch of highway than anywhere else in the country, Jill explained. "The winter here is unpredictable and treacherous." A few winters ago, a minister from Ouray was on this road headed to a Silverton church where he was scheduled to preach. "Everyone advised him not to go." The snow was falling heavily—not a good sign. "But I guess he needed the money or felt the dedication of his calling." The monument she showed us marked the spot where the minister, along with his three young children, perished.

There was a pull-away cut into the mountain where the monument was situated and we considered stopping. But we were already late to meet some friends in Silverton. We had had a late start waiting for Jill's friends, Gail and Diane, who had been delayed. Diane was originally joining us in Jill's Jeep, but when she said she suffered from car sickness, Jill thought that Gail's Beetle was less bumpy, a better car for traveling through the mountains. Diane got into the Beetle with a large empty jar, just in case she got sick. Then five minutes out of town, Jill realized that the person to whom she had lent her Jeep that afternoon had left her with an empty gas tank. So we had had to turn around and come back to Ouray. We waved at Gail and Diane cruising to Silverton, as we headed back.

"There are no guardrails," I said, looking down at the deep bottomless crevice on the side of the road when we later passed the monument.

"The roads are so narrow that the snowplows can't navigate with guardrails," said Jill. "People do get lost—I mean, we lose people. They leave Ouray heading north and they never make it to Silverton."

"You never see them again?"

"Oh, we find them sooner or later, casualties of the mountain."

Jill was smiling and exaggerating, but we all couldn't help thinking about her little joke when we pulled into Silverton to connect with other friends who had left Ouray earlier that day. When we met up with them at Handlebars, a local cowboy bar and restaurant, so named because the bar has numerous photos of patrons sporting handlebar mustaches, we learned that Gail and Diane had not yet arrived.

In fact, they never showed up, and while her friends and guests were drinking beer and wine and speculating about what could have happened to their missing friends, Jill devoted most of her time at Handlebars to calling Gail's cell phone and worrying that she had actually caused her friends to become the casualties she was only recently joking about.

Diane and Gail showed up at breakfast the following morning. As it turned out, Diane had gotten too sick, even in the Beetle, not too long after we passed them as we returned to Ouray. Gail drove her home and they had both gone to bed early.

In retrospect, however, it may have been this dangerous section of roadway and our anxiety of having to traverse it again that actually triggered all of our directional difficulties a few days later.

LEAVING OURAY, Sam and I were relieved to find that we were traveling in the opposite direction and would not have to traverse that dangerous segment of highway again. Before departing and heading to Santa Fe, New Mexico, I consulted MapQuest, which I have discovered to be fairly reliable, although sometimes a bit too anal. If we traveled south on Route 550 from Ouray, I learned, we would eventually connect with I-25, which would take us directly, a straight shot, into Santa Fe. We were meeting a friend in Santa Fe for dinner, time permitting. A hike was scheduled for the following day. The thing is, "south" was Silverton, but I didn't know this at the time.

But when we reached Montrose, Colorado, the town down the mountain from Ouray, I somehow, mysteriously, lost 550. Consulting the map, Sam told me that 550 had ended and that it had turned into Route 50. He directed me back toward 50. I got on it, and we quickly settled in for the comfortable six-hour ride. Harry Potter and Flaming Lips were on the listening agenda.

I actually didn't remember that detail from looking at the map when Sam mentioned it—550 turning into 50—from MapQuest. But I was driving, so I didn't take the time to stop and look at the map again and confirm that detail. But one of the many signs of the way in which old age has overtaken me is my increasing inability to notice what can often be evident and obvious, an unfortunate fact that, in this instance, would come back to haunt me, as it did at the Portal border, when I did not see the sign that told me to wait.

The past few years, Sam has been able to recognize and clarify some obvious details and directions—from maps to manuals to road signs—on my behalf. His eyes notice what mine seem to gloss over—even when it is painfully obvious and literally in front of my eyes and nose. I should say that I still see certain things that Sam cannot see—yet. The way people look, for example. I have learned over the years to walk into a room and scan it—for friendly or familiar faces, for potential foes with shifty eyes, for comfortable corners in which to stand and observe. The subtle stuff. What I seem to miss or find myself unable to focus on is the blatantly obvious.

The Tundra's sound system, for example, has been a challenge from the beginning. The radio is easy. Traditional FM and AM buttons numbered one through six allow programming of twelve separate stations in each band. Loading CDs is also easy: feed the CD into the slot and the player sucks it in. That is as it should be.

But in most vehicles, the radio button numbers, one through six, become the CD numbers. This makes sense. The player holds six CDs. But in the Tundra tiny arrows below numbers three and four indicate the direction to follow when switching from one CD to another. So if you want to switch from CD five to CD two, you press the third button three times. While this is unusual, it isn't rocket science. I could successfully use it after a few coaching sessions from Sam. But since Sam does most of the music selecting and subsequently the CD manipulation, I couldn't remember the arrows or the sequence from one time to another. If I had used the CD player a few times every day, I would have remembered, sooner or later. Repetition works for old people, just like dog trainers use repetition to trick animals to sit, walk, and fetch. A choke collar would have helped me remember, as well. But too much time elapses between playing with the buttons—and my short-term memory lets me down.

Besides, the arrows under the numbers are so small that I can't easily see them. Like I said, my eyes are fine, but I sometimes cannot focus on or recognize the most obvious details. This is an embarrassing fact of my life, which Sam and I have learned to accept about me with quiet good humor. Even the day I missed a one-way sign on a highway and rocketed down a straightaway in the wrong direction turned out, luckily, to be harmless, a momentary mistake.

Generally, I am only slightly annoyed by such synaptic lapses; even I, the control freak, can let these inconsequential matters slip as long as I am able to focus on what I call the "bigger picture." I have always been persistent, always with a goal, a long-range plan, a larger idea. And I rarely, if ever, make a major mistake. "You learn to let the little things slip, if necessary. But you focus on the big stuff and keep it dead center in your scope of awareness until the task is completed," I often preach to Sam. "Never lose sight of the bigger picture. Allow yourself the minor mistakes."

The examples I offered to Sam in this regard related mostly to writing. How a scene, a sentence, or an idea could lead to an essay, a chapter, or even a book. "Every writer starts somewhere; you keep traveling—in this case writing—until you know where you are going. Life (and writing) is more than day-by-day, event-by-event experiences. There's a goal inherent in everything you do. Approach life with an outer eye so that you can get from point A to point B and, simultaneously, an inner eye, a more long-range and sometimes less tangible direction."

So it was easy to assume that Sam had our destination covered. He had the map. Navigation was his job. He was confident, intelligent. I was focusing on the end product, the final destination, the bigger picture.

While we were driving through Montrose, my brother Richard telephoned. He was heading out on his own transcontinental vacation. But after saying goodbye—we had talked maybe fifteen minutes—I suddenly realized we were on the wrong road. Somehow I had gotten turned around and lost Route 50 completely.

Once again, with Sam directing me, we backtracked nine miles to correct ourselves. And then as we drove, eating up the miles on Route 50—it was 330 miles from Ouray to Santa Fe, MapQuest had said—I continued to ask Sam to verify our route and whereabouts, just to make sure. Which he did. Repeatedly. "We're good," he assured me. "Don't worry."

But after a while, I did begin to worry. Something wasn't right. I asked Sam to spread the map out on his lap and put his finger first on Ouray, our starting point, then Santa Fe, our destination, and finally our current location, so that I could be sure we were on track. But as soon as he pointed to the three spots on the map, I immediately realized how wrong we were. I pulled off the road, yanked the map from his lap, and assessed the damage of our miscalculation. I couldn't believe what I was seeing.

I could see in his eyes that Sam recognized our horrible mistake at precisely the same time I did. We were at least a hundred miles—maybe more—further away from our destination than we had been when we had left Ouray three hours ago. I was more than just annoyed. With whom—my son or his dad (me!)—I wasn't certain. This had been such an easy task—just to go from point A to point B. How could we both have gotten it so wrong?

FOR CHRISTMAS, Richard had presented Sam with a mobile GPS receiver, a generous $250 gift. With the supplemental software I purchased for Sam's birthday—an international street atlas—we could track our route and also, when necessary, locate diners for breakfast or the next stop for fuel.

Sam had pointed out that the atlas we had purchased included the entire United States but omitted Canada, essential for the AlCan. Not wanting to limit his learning experience, I purchased more software for an additional $199, pretty much duplicating the atlas, but including Canada. Then Sam and I visited the local AAA office, collected all of the paper maps and guidebooks available for every area of the country through which we were passing, and ordered a Trip Tik, one of those in-depth, turn-by-turn descriptions of recommended routes with maps isolating each part of the area you are driving and the roads to follow highlighted in magic marker.

We put all of this technology and information in a separate Tumi briefcase so that Sam would have easy access and choose a navigational option—paper and/or technology—when the spirit moved him. That Tumi has been with me for two decades, the first real briefcase I ever purchased, for the then-astounding price of $250. It is black—the color of my clothes—and guaranteed indestructible. I had just received tenure at the university where I teach. Buying the Tumi made me feel legitimate and, for the first time in my life, secure. I was then and continued to be the only tenured faculty member throughout the university without an advanced degree. Considering I was a near high school dropout—my guidance counselor had suggested I attend a trade school—tenure and a professorship is a grand achievement.

Why Sam hardly ever opened that Tumi as we traveled through the United States and across Canada on the AlCan, I can't tell you. I can't imagine it has anything to do with the significance of the Tumi, although he was well aware of my checkered and underwhelming past as a former truck driver, traveling shoe salesman, U.S. Coast Guard enlisted man, and all-around basic fat-boy fuck-up. But throughout our weeks on the road, Sam navigated intermittently, relying almost exclusively on the traditional AAA paper map of regions—basically ignoring his GPS.

I did wonder why he was not using his beloved and expensive technology. I asked once or twice, "Why not use the GPS?" Sam replied that he intended to—soon. And while I have come to the parenting game late in life, I have learned through much heartache how to walk the delicate line between guiding a child toward self-discovery and insight and forcing him into something he is reluctant to experience.

But now, we were somewhere in Colorado or New Mexico or God knows where else—totally confused about where we were and what direction we needed to follow next. It's not that we had somewhere special to go and a place to be at a certain time—just that tentative dinner plan, easily postponed or cancelled. But there seemed to be more at stake: pride and ego.

Sitting in the truck that afternoon, we agreed that we were hopelessly lost and confused, but, at the same time, we were both convinced the other person was totally responsible for what had happened to get us so lost. We sat there in the cab of the Tundra, staring at the map, peering sporadically out the window at the unmarked crossroads to our left and right, our confusion and frustration rapidly snowballing.

The Big Picture

SUDDENLY, ALL OF THE self-control I had nurtured, all of the wise counsel I had heaped upon myself about being the good, calm, reflective, understanding dad—the dad of whom I had dreamed and felt certain I could emulate—went flying out the window. It was like a rope, burning my hands while I was falling but unable to stop myself. Fight back fear and anger, I heard myself thinking. Control your emotions and control of the situation will follow. But I was helpless. "Sam," I bellowed, "how could you?"

Startled by my explosive eruption, and by the question itself, as if he had done something on purpose to hurt me, Sam began to shriek and cry, "I don't know, I don't know, I don't know!"

Our world of order, dialogue, and thoughtful intelligence, of which I had been so proud, shattered right before our eyes. I yelled again and again. I don't remember what I said. Probably just repeated what I had been saying, "How could you? How could you?" And Sam was shrieking even more hysterically. I remember one other time when this happened—a point when I had totally lost control. This was some years ago. I had purchased a bike rack for my Ford Explorer SUV, which was mounted on top of the roof rack. It was so high I needed a small stepladder to lock the bikes on top. We were heading east to attend a wedding.

There are four tunnels along the Pennsylvania Turnpike from Pittsburgh to Philadelphia, and that day, Sam and I had a terrific time speculating about the low clearance limits for each of them and the likelihood that we would make it to New Jersey with our bikes and roof rack intact. Interestingly, we were unable to locate low clearance warning signs at the entrances to some of the tunnels, but hours later, I clearly saw the sign hanging on a chain suspended from the ceiling as I entered the Atlantic City Holiday Inn parking garage—LOW CLEARANCE: SIX FEET EIGHT INCHES—and I ignored it, thinking that the posted clearance seemed unnecessarily low. Or maybe I thought that the signs and the rules simply did not apply to me.

I figured I could easily drive up the ramp unfettered. And I almost did. The Explorer cruised untouched from the first to the second level—until we collided loudly, sickeningly, with two ceiling pipes that I had believed we could slip under. I stopped, took a deep breath, closed my eyes, counted to ten—and then when I became aware of the reality of my humiliating and thoughtless action in front of my son, I totally lost my composure. I began punching the steering wheel and yelling "Stupid! Stupid! Stupid!" Even as I was in the middle of my tantrum, I couldn't believe that I was acting so foolishly, but I literally couldn't help myself.

I jumped out of the Explorer to inspect the damage: the pipe had sliced my bike's seat in half. I felt lucky. Bike seats were inexpensive, relatively—and, most importantly, Sam's bike was untouched. At that point, I was so embarrassed that I had displayed such poor judgment in front of Sam, and then had lost my composure, that I just wanted to get the experience over with. Maybe take a swim in the ocean and redeem myself in my son's eyes. And I wanted to demonstrate that my judgment wasn't that faulty and that I had made just one tiny miscalculation, and in the end everything would be all right. It was only a ruined bike seat, after all. Daddy's bike seat—not Sam's.

So without looking for any additional obstruction, I jumped back into the Explorer, started the engine, put it into gear, stomped on the accelerator—and immediately smashed into another water pipe—the last remaining pipe between me and the top of the ramp. Now both bikes clattered to the ground and the water pipe with which I had collided was torn from its anchor on the ceiling. It was bending precariously, as if it were about to break and burst. I paused to assess the situation—and to take a deep breath.

I tried to imagine what Winston Churchill might do at a moment like this or how he would advise his people. But smashing into a pipe in a parking garage had nothing to do with tenacity or dedication; it had much more to do with clarity of thought and self-respect—or the sudden lack of them. I wanted so much to be able to escape the embarrassment of the situation in front of Sam and to survive with some dignity, but instead of rallying to the moment, falling down nine times and getting up ten, "never giving up and never giving in," as Churchill proclaimed, I suddenly, in defiance of whatever dignity I had remaining, began to cry. And when I felt the heat of the tears in my eyes, I began punching the steering wheel one more time and I heard myself yelling, even louder than the first time, "Stupid! Stupid! Stupid!" Sitting in that car, punching the steering wheel, yelling and screaming and feeling nakedly foolish, I remember thinking, "This is the worst moment of my life." And it was—at least until I went stark raving stupidly mad during our ride from Ouray to Santa Fe.

The low clearance bike incident happened a long time ago, as I said. But I can see the surprise in Sam's face and hear the startled helplessness even now, as I write this. It is the same horror and surprise that reflected in his face and eyes as we sat in the Tundra on the side of the road that afternoon.

We must have both realized—simultaneously—how ugly we were acting—how inappropriately out of control—how surreal we sounded, and, in an instant, we descended into a deafening, eerie silence. Sitting on the shoulder of the highway—the wrong highway—listening to the whooshing roar of the cars and trucks as they rocketed by and the persistent blinking of my emergency flashers, we both stared down at the map trying to get ourselves under enough control to assess the situation with clarity and to figure out, in no particular order, where we were, exactly, and how we could find the most prudent route back to our initial destination.

My frustration and anger at Sam's mistake and his fear of my explosive rage and his embarrassment wafted in the Tundra's cab like glue. Somehow we had gone way off course; I was losing sight of my coveted bigger picture—and my confidence in myself.

Antelope Galloping

FIVE DAYS BEFORE, on our way to Ouray, the mere possibility of a similar blunder had also unhinged me. Talking on the telephone as I sat in the truck in the parking lot of the Hilton Garden Inn in Elko, Nevada, a friend said, "I thought you were supposed to be in Ouray this evening. "No," I told her, "Tomorrow evening."

"I was looking at your website. I thought for sure it was today."

"No," I repeated. "Tomorrow night." I was confident.

But later, halfway through dinner at a restaurant adjacent to a nearby casino, I began to believe my friend was right and that I had made a major miscalculation.

I rushed Sam through dinner and drove at top speed back to the motel to rifle through my papers. After five frantic minutes, I found the papers that I needed and scanned through them until I realized I was right. I should have known. I might miss a few minute details of my complicated life, but these big mistakes I don't normally make— until now.

It took just a minute to understand how Sam could have consistently confirmed our route and simultaneously been so extraordinarily mistaken. I had told Sam that we were to follow 550 most of the way and that it would eventually run into I-25 which would take us to Santa Fe. I asked him to make certain the plan made sense. When he saw that 550 ended and turned into 50, he assumed I misspoke, and that I meant 50 and not 550. This is a mistake I will often make: calling something one thing and meaning something else. I was constantly forgetting exact names of teachers, friends, streets, and numbers. "Whatever," I would say after he would correct me, "you know what I mean."

So it was easy to think that he could intuit or interpret my route. Route 50 instead of 550 was close enough in "Dad-speak." And when he followed 50 with his finger on the map across Colorado it did in fact lead to I-25, which, in turn, plunged down through Colorado and into New Mexico, connecting to Santa Fe. It seemed right. So Sam did not consider the situation any further. He did not realize that this route, albeit correct, would take us twice as long.

What we had to do now was to focus on how to get back on the right track. Sometimes the most horrific and ridiculous mistakes can lead to ideas and adventures that would have been otherwise impossible. Parked on the side of the road in the middle of Route 50, nowhere near a town or a marker to help us locate ourselves, we found the thin line of a secondary road on our map. Route 114 connected to 285, which would take us directly into Santa Fe. It wouldn't eradicate our hundred-mile mistake, but it might help make up a little time.

How to get to 114 from the middle of nowhere was another matter—until a man and a woman in a Jeep stopped near us to establish their own whereabouts. They had just followed a narrow, winding dirt road of enchanting vistas and exciting twists and turns that had delighted them, they told us—the same dirt road, it turned out after examining their area map, that would, with a few modifications, lead us to 114. Everything they told us about the mysterious dirt road turned out to be true. We cruised in a dramatic cloud of red dust for twenty miles, pausing frequently to drink in the lonely vista of plain dotted with prickly lodge-pole pine and grazing cattle, swirling wind-swept red dust and hulking mountains, shadowed in hues of black and blue. The experience was awe-inspiring, not just because of the spare, stark beauty, but in the way life surprises and reveals how despair and anger can, suddenly, amazingly, lead to hope and pleasure.

At one point, two antelopes appeared from nowhere, exploding out of the trees and galloping in all their graceful majesty alongside our truck. Then, as I struggled to slow down to avoid hitting or frightening them, they darted in front of us. For an instant, we were on a collision course. But the sweetness of their surprise appearance and the startling beauty of their gait suspended and muted the evident danger until the crisis resolved itself without much effort and the antelope disappeared into the trees on the other side of the red dust road.

The power of our antelope encounter made us both breathless. I stopped the Tundra so that I could take a photograph of Sam in front of the spot into which the antelope had disappeared. Then Sam and I hugged and kissed, cheek to cheek. I was so moved, I felt like crying.

This was a moment to forever cherish. I felt so lucky to have such a loving and forgiving child and the freedom to be with him in the middle of nowhere, in a place like paradise. If God exists—a question that I seem to be asking with more regularity and persistence, He was, at that moment, enveloping us.

Later, safe and sound on 114, Sam and I discussed and laughed about how fortunate we were to have made such an extraordinary blunder. The mountain road and the galloping antelope—they had come so close to us they had almost kissed our truck—would not have existed had we paid more attention to the map or consulted our GPS. "This was real truckin'" Sam said, "going with the flow."

But I was able to isolate a more satisfying reward: the way in which we had made peace after our initial explosive temperamental outbursts. Usually we stay angry for longer periods after such monumental goof-ups. Not angry, exactly. We require a cooling-off period—a few minutes of silence to clear heads and calm our nerves. One of the profound achievements of my life, especially since the coming of Sam, has been my ability to tame my temperamental outbursts. I may scream for fifteen seconds, but then, rather quickly, I can talk and be rational.

But in this instance, I made the transition immediately, with good reason. Studying the map, I recognized the fatal flaw in my mistake. The incident that triggered the entire experience, although elongated and complicated by Sam, had started with me. My inner eye, resting on the bigger picture, that major mistake I worked so hard to not allow myself to make, had occurred. The line of error to which I was so dedicated and determined not to cross had been violated.

Sitting in the truck that day in the middle of Route 50, feeling strained and momentarily bereft, and steaming inside and out at Sam, I looked at the map a second and third time, trying to understand how we had gotten so completely turned around. Clarity came eventually, followed by my own searing humiliation.

Sam, well aware that I was prone to small mistakes—never the big ones—had done his best to adjust to the direction I had chosen and to follow my usually reliable lead. But this time my efforts had fallen short. His confidence had been radically misplaced. For I realized, as I studied the map, that when we left Ouray that morning to follow 550 south and east to Santa Fe, I had gone north and west. I had, in other words, started us off by making the basic mistake, going in the wrong direction. Everything that happened after that that went wrong was my fault. Sam figured out how to follow 50 to I-25 to Santa Fe, an incredibly roundabout route, but totally true to my initial directions and wishes.

This was probably the second most telling and jarring example of how children turn the tables on their parents—the moment when you, the parent, see the balance of power shifting, when role reversals occur. At one point you are the supreme being. The big and most powerful dad, the real macho man. The Sensei. You know everything. Your child knows little and he hangs on your every word. Whatever you say, your son respects and believes.

Gradually, though, your son begins to acquire knowledge and strength. He is catching up with you. The father is not necessarily going backwards. He is not losing knowledge and strength in middle age. It just becomes more difficult to maintain the façade of superiority—until he can no longer keep up, not necessarily because he is getting slower—but because his offspring overtakes him. This is as it should be. Alas. This is the painful and illuminating truth I discovered at the Exit Glacier summit.

Paul and Barbara

From Sam's Journal:

Soldotna. That's where we ended up after the Writers' Conference—at the privately owned Timber Wolf Lodge.

We got into our room, the Silver Salmon room; here, the rooms were not numbered, instead they were named with fishes. I was happy with the room. My dad was not: he said it was dirty and uncomfortable. But I liked the way the room was: an acceptable bathroom, two bunk beds, and a larger regular bed. I took the top bunk while Dad took the larger bed. This arrangement worked well, making the bottom bunk accessible for storage. I thought the bunk was comfortable, although the sheets were somewhat dirty; it was nice, like our base in Alaska where we got ready for whatever we were going to do.

We could buy groceries because it had a kitchen and it was easily accessible—first floor. It also had weather gauges, which was interesting because most rooms do not have things like that. It had an empty refrigerator and cupboards with dishes. It was a nice stay and a good stopping point for our hike up Exit Glacier.

AT THE FOOT OF Exit Glacier, on the road out of Seward, Alaska, peering up at that massive slab of ice and snow squeezed between two jagged black and white mountains, you can't help thinking about the way the world was formed and is now changing. The melting muddy gray water, icy and thick, tumbling into deep pools, is the first evidence of the glacier gradually devouring itself. Then, as you continue into

Kenai Fjords National Park and up the winding spur road to the trail-
head, you see signs marking how far the glacier has receded in the past
half-century—from 1952 it's a mile up to 1978, then a mile more to
1995—a not-so-subtle and hauntingly measurable impact of global
warming.

In Anchorage and the other towns we have passed through, kids
have set up lemonade stands to quench the thirst of overheated travelers. The newspapers are filled with stories. Ice cream is melting in
freezers. Lawns and gardens are being watered twice a day. By the end
of the summer, Anchorage, the state capital, will have tied the record
for most days over 70 degrees—43. The last time there were so many
70-plus days was 1936. Alaska is capable of getting even hotter: the
highest temperature ever recorded was 100 degrees in Fort Yukon on
June 27, 1915.

DURING THE MONTHS of preparation for our Alaska trip, Kathy, my
friend from Soldotna, just north of Homer, beseeched us to bring warm
clothing, and I have gone out of my way to heed her warnings and prepare, with expensive rain suits, down vests, extra sweaters. But what we
really need now is sunscreen. A few days ago, I went to the desk clerk at
the Land's End Resort in Homer, in the Kenai Peninsula where we are
staying, complaining that the air conditioning didn't work in my room.

"Sir," he said, looking at me incredulously, "this is Alaska. We don't
have air conditioning."

"But the thermostat on the wall has a setting for 'cool' and goes
down to 60 degrees," I protested.

"That's because thermostats are made for people in the lower 48,"
the man sneered. "We learn to adapt in Alaska."

THE MOSQUITOES attacked the moment we started up the trail, an
army lying in wait to ambush and destroy us. I was glad I had heeded
Kathy's warning to take plenty of bug dope, which I sprayed generously
all over us. Sam made an "I'm being tortured, leave me alone face" and
kept turning away as I sprayed his cheeks and forehead. "This smells
terrible," he complained.

"That's what we hope the mosquitoes are saying to themselves,"
Kathy said, punching the air like a shadow boxer to drive the buzzing
beasts away. "'I can't stand the smell—I give up. I'll leave these poor
people alone and bother somebody else.'"

The flies are super-sized in Alaska, but the mosquitoes are more
oppressive. Forget the bug dope on a walk in the woods, as we did two
days later at the Soldotna Nature Center, and return with itching

pulsing welts all over your face, neck, and arms—the scars of your mistake. The wasps are also prevalent, dive-bombing into your eyes and terrorizing you.

As we climbed higher up Exit Glacier, the mosquitoes became less of a problem and by the time we reached the snow, they had totally disappeared, not reappearing until many hours later, during our descent.

Of the three of us, the least prepared person was Kathy, the Alaskan, who went on this hike with leaky boots. While Sam and I stomped through the snow in our waterproof, insulated Gore-Tex hikers, Kathy sloshed through puddles, swearing at her boots and vowing to destroy them the moment she returned home. Exit Glacier, in the Kenai Mountains, was named because it served as the "exit" for the first recorded crossing of the Harding Ice Fields, which was where we were headed, at the summit.

Most Alaskans who live near Exit Glacier, one of the most scenic hikes in the country, have never actually seen the Harding Ice Field, despite a great many accessible hiking trails. Some people we talked with had attempted it and stopped because of bad weather, or because they had taken some friends and relatives—out of shape or unprepared outsiders from the lower 48—who had, for various reasons, not been able to go all the way.

Not climbing Exit Glacier is, for Alaskans, something like living in Manhattan all your life and never visiting the Statue of Liberty or the top of the Empire State Building. Unless you have guests to entertain, people tend to their business or personal lives and assume that, since it is so accessible to them, they will get to it in time. They don't.

The Exit Glacier ascent was the event Sam and I had been anticipating the most, the highlight of the trip, for it was going to be our macho experience, just like the Grand Canyon had been the macho challenge of the previous truckin' year, when we had our Ranger. I think that this is a "man thing." Guys have to have goals; we just can't just do things just for the fun of it. There's got to be a rationale and a challenge, something or somebody to compete with and to beat.

Last year, there was one point in our trek into Havasu Canyon when I knew Sam was going to be all right. We were coming into Havasu Village, the home of the Havasupai Indians ("Havasupai" means "people of the blue-green waters"), the smallest Indian nation in America, totaling about six hundred people. This was after starting at Havasu Hilltop (5199 elev.) three hours earlier and walking eight miles to the canyon floor in 106-degree heat. We were at the outskirts of the village and Sam was beginning to wilt, whine and become irritable. He was angry and wouldn't talk with me. I said, "Sam, you assured me you could do this when I tried to talk with you about it yesterday. So just get yourself back together; I'm holding you to your promise."

Sam didn't say anything at that point, but he abruptly moved out ahead of me, without a word. A mile later when we stopped for lunch and he ate his favorite meal, grilled cheese—the cheese sandwich that had been grilled or boiled inside my backpack so that it tasted something like Elmer's Glue, he grinned at me, his braces glittering in the sun. "Sam is revived," he said.

The other boy we joined up with on this trek, thirteen-year-old Paul, would never revive—or perhaps he wasn't allowed to. By the time we reached the village he was tired and grumbling about the heat and extended exertion. But Paul didn't seem particularly spent—no more than the rest of us. How many people can walk a steep downhill over a dicey, rocky terrain in 100-plus degree heat for three hours, virtually nonstop, without feeling the effects? In retrospect, I believe, this was the pivotal point at which to set a tone and make a statement for Paul—quietly but firmly—just as I did with Sam. Why it didn't happen has a lot to do with the differences between men and women and mothers and fathers and the delicate balance that must be sustained in relation to how they, dad or mom, relate to and respond to their sons.

As we paused for lunch that day, Paul's mom, Barbara, told everyone that Paul had been unhappy about this trek from the start. They were on a one-month holiday together; Paul's elder brother had gone off to Europe to visit relatives with his father, and his elder sister was also in Europe, traveling with friends. "Paul is stuck with me," she said.

That Paul didn't want to hike or climb is not clear. Given the choice at the beginning when the trip was being planned, he might have declined. But he seemed a moderately fit young man of average height and weight. And he shot down the mountain for eight miles ahead of us all before the heat got to him. Even then, he hiked two more miles to our campsite and then accompanied us to Havasu Falls for a swim. A little encouragement is what he needed—perhaps more than just encouragement—a push. But Barbara was not inclined to push—without pulling at the same time.

Barbara went down the mountain without hesitation, although she continued to discuss her weak knees as a way of explaining why she was always behind everyone else. She was a woman of around forty-five, moderately overweight—and talkative. But she was good-humored and a caring mother. But for her son, she was perhaps the wrong person at the wrong place and time. Throughout the rest of the trek in Havasu Canyon, Sam and I and the other members of our group hiked long distances, climbed rocks, diving into the many pristine pools made by the majestic waterfalls pouring into the Colorado River; we played like children, with abandon.

Barbara and Paul stayed close to our campsite, not accompanying us and the other four members of the group we had joined. Eventually, Barbara rented horses in the village for she and Paul to ride the miles back up to the canyon summit. We never saw them again. And we all sympathized with Paul, who had been dragged into an experience he had preferred to not be a part of—and then not to be allowed a chance to make the best of it. That wasn't fair.

What can we conclude about all of this, if anything? That men need to compete and women need to protect? I think that this may be a safe generalization, although we could devote a month to the exceptions to the rule. Competition and winning are male traits, but so too are protecting and preserving what he owns and loves. Women are quite competitive, especially against other women, although not often as shamelessly as men. Women are also more cautious, like Barbara, which can sometimes be annoying to the men and boys they are with.

From Sam's Journal:

Living in the woods at Havasu Canyon was a little bit hard. No music. No computer. No running water. No shower (well, at first that's good). No clean toilet. Bugs. And the tents boiled over at night. They were extremely hot. We didn't have a fan. And my special pillow was absent too. On the other hand, living in the woods was fun. The camp was pretty nice. The people were nice. Living casually was fun. Our adventures were fun.

Then there was Barbara. My Dad and I talked a bit about this. On the second day, when we were supposed to go exploring together, she backed out with Paul. On the fourth day, Barbara again chickened out and decided to either ride a horse back or get a helicopter back. She said she couldn't make it up the hill. I think that while we were swimming in Beaver Falls, exploring with the group, they were buying a ride back. I felt bad for Paul. What was wrong with Barbara?

Bears on the Brain

ON OUR WAY UP Exit Glacier, we met two Pittsburghers, now living in Virginia and working for the U.S. Postal Service. We chatted briefly about hometowns, neighborhoods we once lived in, and the beloved Steelers, the world's most famous football team and Pittsburgh's most significant claim to fame now that the steel industry has faded. Unlike the Steelers, a team known for its grit and determination to plow ahead against all obstacles, no matter how menacing, these Pittsburghers had decided—abruptly—to curtail their Exit Glacier hike and retreat back down the trail toward their car.

"The bears spooked her," the man said, nodding at his wife. He pointed backward. "They're right up around the bend, feeding in a meadow, and when she saw them, she was too afraid to go further."

We were wary when we heard about the bears, but canceling this hike because of a bear sighting was hardly in the cards, not after coming so far and working so hard to get here. Besides, Kathy said, bears are less likely to attack humans in such a well-traveled part of the trail; there might be more to worry about, bear-wise, as we continued to climb higher, but there's too much traffic here to be afraid.

We saw the bears a few minutes later. Two cubs and a mama black bear (or two medium-sized adolescents, depending on who you talked with; I think I saw three, but Kathy and Sam will only attest to two) surrounded by their own private admiration society and cheering section. At least a dozen hikers were standing on a ledge behind a thicket peering down into a meadow in which the bears were feeding on shrubs and berries. I say "cheering" section because the group was making so much noise whispering to one another, unbuckling their backpacks and knapsacks and digging for their cameras and then clicking, while motioning for us to be quiet as we approached them while clicking some more, that the bears would have to have been anesthetized not have noticed us.

Bears. If you want to engage an Alaskan in conversation, get a perfect stranger talking, nonstop, then invoke the B word. Bears in the backyard, bears in the highway, bears in the street, bears on top of your car are stories that trigger rapt attention and debate at dinners, cocktail parties, and grocery stores. There are black bears in Alaska, which are relatively small, perhaps three hundred pounds at the most, and grizzlies, which can weigh nearly half a ton and reach a height of nearly thirteen feet when they rear up on their hind legs (which they often do). Grizzlies are called brown bears in southwestern Alaska, misleading people into assuming that there are three kinds of bears in Alaska. There are only two. The term "grizzly" was first used during the Lewis and Clark expedition, in reference to a brown bear with a "grizzled appearance." Sam and I saw a great many grizzlies during our sixteen-hundred-mile sprint up the AlCan. The bears we were watching on the way up toward Exit Glacier were black bears—small, in fact—and for a second we joined the group to observe with rapt attention.

Bears are so compelling, in some ways, hypnotic to outsiders and natives alike. Here in Alaska, newspapers burst with bear stories. The week we were visiting the Kenai, the big event was a bear attacking and devouring a moose cub in the driveway of a house in suburban Anchorage, while the mother moose stood by, prudently sacrificing her child's life for her own. The mauling was videotaped by the owner of the house and rerun repeatedly on each newscast, like the famous O. J. Simpson car chase, on TV. But curiously, no one had called the police. Nor did anyone think that not calling the police was a fact worth noting. "What could the police do?" Kathy asked.

"Kill the bear," I said.

"That's not their job."

"So did anyone call the Wildlife Department?" I asked.

"What for? Bears are a way of life here."

On the one hand, bear stories and bear paranoia abound. Bears on the brain in Alaska. Yet, people are also blasé about bears.

When we were there, the most often repeated bear story was about an amateur documentary filmmaker, Timothy Treadwell, who threw caution to the wind to get up close and cozy with bears, insisting that he had a special way with bears, knew how to reach and captivate them. His first film about bears was an award-winner, and when he returned to Alaska for a follow-up project, he became even bolder and more adventuresome by setting up his cameras in the Katmai National Park, an area known for its abundant bear population, and waiting brazenly with the camera and his girlfriend, Amy Hugenard, a physician's assistant, for the bears to approach and perform. Which they did one afternoon.

Fortunately the video portion of the cameras the filmmaker had set up to turn on automatically when the bears walked into the clearing had malfunctioned, but unfortunately, the audio remained to the bitter end, recording in precise word-for-word, scream-for-scream detail the bears' attack on both the filmmaker and his girlfriend and their slow and agonizing demise as the bears, one by one, first the filmmaker and then the girlfriend, devoured them in October 2003. Sam and I saw the movie "Grizzly Man," produced and directed by Werner Herzog, using Treadway's raw footage, a year after we visited Alaska.

Lorrie McCarthy, the Forest Service Naturalist on the ferry *Columbia*, told us that bears could smell an intruder a quarter of a mile away and hear the click of a camera the length of a football field. Which is exactly why Kathy was so nervous on Exit Glacier.

"Let's get outta here while the getting is good," Kathy whispered. "The bears are great to watch, but I prefer escaping with my arms and legs intact." We sprinted up the trail and around the bear groupies and kept on climbing.

Winning (and Losing) the Race

THE FIRST PART of the hike up the glacier was slow and steep. We were soon overheated and soaked with perspiration. Kathy peeled off her jacket, but Sam and I continued to climb in our windbreakers, sweating onward until we hit the snow, which gradually, as we climbed, helped cool us off.

Overdressing—too many clothes in warm weather—is a Lee Gutkind trademark. I have far too many things to carry—notebook, pen, wallet (and sometimes a digital camera or tape recorder)—so I desperately need pockets. I don't have anything against purses for men, but that too is something extra, and it seems easier to wear these items then have to dig around for them in a backpack.

In the U.S. Coast Guard, our dress-blue wool jumpers were pocketless; wrinkles and bulges were prohibited. Bell-bottom trousers fit tight around the waist with a single back pocket for wallets. Those Zippo lighters we all carried fit perfectly in the traditional sailor's watch pocket, but where were a seaman's cigarettes? In a very handy and yet unlikely hideaway: the bands of our socks, hugging our ankles! I don't smoke anymore, but my cell phone is perhaps a more serious addiction. Even on the glacier, I could feel its soothing presence, pressed tightly against my ankle above the tops of my hiking boot, right where my cigarettes once were.

The terrain leveled off as we climbed, but the snow got deeper, burying our boots, cloaking our ankles, numbing our knees. This was not powder but wet and heavy snow. Untouched and unsoiled. Slippery. Then, when we were within a mile or so of the summit, the terrain got steeper.

At first, we were able to follow a trail of tiny orange flags marked by a Park Service ranger, but the flags soon disappeared, and we had to bushwhack our own way, our general direction guided by the far-off distant summit, a sparkling mass of glittering white, caked with ice blue. There were many trails—just lines of footprints, really—but none that seemed most suitable to follow. After slipping, sliding, and falling in and out of other hikers' mistakes, we realized that braving our way through new snow, although colder and deeper, would work best. But it was slow going. Three steps forward meant two steps sliding backward. The trick was to keep your legs moving, continue to scramble upward, often on all fours, in order to maintain a slow and steady forward progress. And this is where I became my most effective and obnoxious self.

Something happens to me when I get into situations like this, a combination of panic and sheer persistence, jelling, building, converging, and exploding. A time to be tested: against the elements, against other people, and against myself. My heart beats faster and I click into a special awareness and focus on the task ahead, an intense tunnel vision emerges within me that allows me to block out any extraneous details and hone in on my overall objective, as in the case of the rising plain of snow confronting us.

I feel this adrenalin burst when I write; I can feel it now, as I climb. Each step is like a sentence for an essay, each double step a paragraph, each triple step a page—before I slide back down and start again. That's what writing and my life are all about: starting, stopping, gaining momentum, falling back and fighting forward. *Failing*, inevitably, at first, and then just as inevitably, trying again to succeed. *Failing*, but progressing, establishing a goal, an eye on the bigger picture, maintaining a vision toward a triumphant end.

"Fall down nine times and get up ten," is the phrase I continue to press upon Sam.

"Never give up," I say, pushing the concept further by paraphrasing Winston Churchill, "Never give in, never give up. Never. Never. Never. Ever." I don't claim to live up to these philosophical platitudes every day of my life, but I'm constantly pushing everyone I know to do more than they think they can do or want to do. I become crazed. Like now, I am always going for the summit.

All the while I have in my mind the bigger picture—the top of the mountain or the hill—or the end of the scene I am writing or the accomplishment of my goal. That is the never-give-in, never-give-up, fall-down-nine-times-get-up-ten philosophy I am constantly haranguing Sam with.

As I move forward in this manner, working feverishly against the frustration and challenge of the hill, legs churning, three steps forward and two steps back, I become increasingly crazed. The juice of the repressed energy I am whipping up pours into me like a narcotic and drives me even faster, narrowing and invigorating the focus of the objective. I can't control it.

I am not self-destructive. I don't jump out of airplanes or windsurf, but I hunger for situations offering an edge, and then I try to see what it takes—what inner resources I will have to muster forth—to meet the challenge and beat it. Invariably, I disconnect from the world around me, and I am suddenly in my own space—like a meteor rocketing toward the earth, crashing through the atmosphere with thundering spark and fire and colliding explosively with the ground.

This is the most enlightening and invigorating feeling. While I don't lose an awareness of time, distance, or other people—the practicalities are lodged in my mind—the adrenalin releases me. Facing the slope of snow and feeling myself gearing up to overpower it, I knew that Kathy was minding Sam for the moment, so I could permit this explosion of expression.

Kathy had started the hike with a vigorous pace that Sam and I had struggled initially to keep up with. But now, I rocketed off, leaving her way behind. First I was fighting for and finding a path in the snow, rediscovering remnants of dry land in the trail, crashing through other fields of snow, moving faster and faster. Then I began running. In my hiking boots, my daypack bouncing on my back, it was like plunging through the obstacle course at Coast Guard boot camp all over again, forty years later. I was crazed.

Suddenly, I was young, strong, driven. The distance between Sam and Kathy and I began to lengthen. After a while, I lost sight of them. I knew that Kathy was slowing down and tiring and I realized that my responsibility, Sam, was behind me, and I had to stop acting so crazily, so wild. But I couldn't help myself. At one point I heard Kathy, her voice shallow and distant, flagged by the wind. "Lee, wait! Slow down!"

When I get like this, I am unstoppable. I am in another world, energized and magnetized and jet-propelled. As I have gotten older, this feeling—the experiencing of massive explosions of adrenalin—has become less prevalent. This is because of age, but also I think I have less to prove to myself these days. I am not so angry at the world anymore.

While I don't hunger for the return of the hostility I have harbored in the past, I don't like this lack of fire in me. In a way, I miss the ongoing battles against authority figures—bosses, parents, elders, etc.—my tendency to see enemies and whip up conflict in every direction, and my hunger for achievement and reinforcement no matter what the cost. So when it happens, when I get carried away with something, like the fight over the slippery slope of snow to get to the top of Exit Glacier, I relive the feelings of fight from the past—the fire and passion and even the mystery and frustration of youth—and I know once again, physically, I am nearly unbeatable, as evidenced by Kathy, perhaps fifteen years younger than me, gasping and screaming in my crazed wake.

Finally, I forced myself to slow down, taking back some control over my actions. I was feeling guilty for leaving behind my friend and host, not to mention my son, but I was also glowing inside with an aura of triumph. I could still beat most people, I thought. I could still marshal my amazing ability to concentrate with all of my physical resources and demonstrate my superiority and my grit over anybody, almost. I was ecstatic with this thought. I was screaming my elation to myself. But then came the sound and movement, which I first sensed and then heard: distinct footsteps behind me. I turned. Sam.

The realization that Sam had caught up with me—me at my strongest, my most powerful and supercharged best—was startling. For years I had been the person pushing Sam and setting the pace for him—I still was, I knew, and would be for a few more years, but I could see now that he really didn't need me as much anymore and would soon not need me at all. Like any son, he was catching up with his father. Bypassing me was inevitable.

This is something that sons keep in the back of their minds. At least I had always been thinking about it with a certain glint of anticipation and satisfaction as I entered and exited my teenage years. That my own father would not always be so strong and overpowering compared to me, and that slowly but surely I would creep up and catch him, and that I would, through sheer endurance, overpower and overtake that obnoxious bastard, that dirty, torturing son-of-a-bitch, who taunted and drove me.

And then when it happened, when my father was finally dying in the hospital and I was bending over his bed, my lips soaking-in his final breath, I could only envision my son, Sam, hovering over me in a similarly awkward manner.

What will my son be feeling as I lay dying?

Will he remember our triumphant ascent of Exit Glacier, of how we stood together, holding hands, overlooking that sparkling blue sea of ice and crystal?

Will this image, this magic moment, burn in his mind and tattoo his heart with the legacy of my unyielding commitment to survival and achievement—to what I have tried to teach him about life? To doing his best? To never relenting? To always be over-achieving? To finding and following a vision?

Or will I lose my son to my own obsession to overcome everyone and everything and prevail? Will he look at me and decide, thinking back, that I am a fake and a phony, that I am pushy, insecure? That I am an old man, pretending, trying to stay and act young, but slipping? A lightweight? A blowhard? All the things I fear I am, will he come to believe that that is me?

The Summit

I WAITED FOR Kathy to catch up. We sat for a while as she ate a hard-boiled egg and rested. A few hikers who had made it to the summit and were now descending encouraged us to move forward and not give up. "There's a hut near the summit, less than a mile from here. Then five minutes after the hut is the greatest vista you have ever seen," one man told us.

We moved on, slogging through the slush on the trail and periodically fighting our way through the new snow. I apologized to Kathy for running away. "I get carried away," I said.

"It's alright," she replied. "Everybody gets carried away in Alaska."

The summit was, as promised, spellbinding. From a nub barely the size of a garage, we stood overlooking the gray slab of the glacier we had climbed at the edge of the sparkling blue sheet of the Harding Ice Field. It was a magnificent sight, but, more than that, we shared the triumphant joy of achievement. "Sam," said Kathy, "you did it! You climbed a glacier."

Sam's bursting smile, the victorious glow on his face that is now registered in mind and memory, is what I have been working for, what, in fact, I think is the special gift I can give my son. It is what I owe him and want to instill in him: not to be afraid of challenge, of taking on difficult leaps, of attempting to do great things. *Most anything is possible if you work hard enough* is my message to my son, and the hard work will be worthwhile, as evidenced by the triumphant feeling, this magic moment of achievement at the edge of the Harding Ice Field in the

middle of Alaska when he is only thirteen years old, at the beginning of what I am hoping will become a glorious life.

Sam's Journal:

The best part was what we did next. On Wednesday, we climbed Exit Glacier. It was a good hike, climbing mountains via rocks and boards and flags and descending carefully through snow. We were all prepared, except Kathy, who had non-waterproof boots. The bug dope worked for us all, until the end, when it began to wear off. The snow was annoying, climbing up was difficult because with almost every step you took, you would slide down somewhat, and the extreme brightness and whiteness of the snow would be difficult to look at. But when we got to the top, it was great. The shelter was very small and had only one small room. And up here the snow was not flagged where the trail was, making the decision your own. We sat down in a place overlooking the Harding Ice Field, sitting on a place where there was no snow, eating and relaxing. What could be better?

Old Men

COMING DOWN THE mountain was easier and faster than up. But it was more harrowing and angst producing. Navigating the slippery snow was worrisome; we were slipping, falling, and sliding. Sam was tiring, I could tell, and his anxiety was building. Midway, working our way down through the dense snowfield we had scrambled up, a hiker, a girl who had passed us going up, was now stalled, sprawled on all fours, filled with trepidation and afraid to move for fear of falling. Her young husband—I found out later that they were newlyweds who had come to Alaska from Chicago to get married—stood in front of her, offering her his hand. "What do you want me to do?" he said.

"Stay with me," she said. "I don't know anything else to tell you. That's all I need."

"You can't just stay there in the middle of the mountain," he pleaded.

"I know," she said. She was crying.

Exasperated, her husband shrugged and dropped down in the snow. The newlyweds shook off our offer of help, so we kept going.

By the time we got halfway through the snow, Sam was getting tense. Like the woman trapped in the middle of the snowfield, the precariousness of the situation—not having traction, control—was making him nervous and hesitant. And then when we finally worked our way through the snow, the steep rocky crevices we had climbed up were surprisingly harrowing going down, now that we were tiring and in a hurry to finish. Sam was wearing out. I could tell he was beginning to panic. He was becoming impatient and losing his concentration.

"Hang in, Sam," I said.

"I'm tired," he said.

"You can't let yourself give in to the tiredness," I said. "You're strong. You can't be beaten down," I tried to rally him. "Buck up!"

"I can't." Now he was whining; his voice was tearful and shrill, causing Kathy to hesitate, turn around and look at us.

"Keep your voice down," I said sharply. "You're losing it."

"Don't talk to me that way, dad," Sam immediately replied, turning around to confront me. "Don't tell me what to say. And don't tell me how loud I should talk."

I stared at him in silence, watching Kathy out of the corner of my eye. I didn't want her to know that we were having a disagreement—that there was ever any friction between Sam and me. She was my former student and a protégé, and although I am certain she did not think I was perfect, I wanted her to feel as if I was someone special—someone worthy of following and modeling herself after. Being a great mentor is part and parcel of being a great father. There would be no chinks in my armor, at least in public, if I could help it.

So many students in my life, like the little twenty-four-year-old from the writers' conference, who called me sensei—literally dozens of young people (some, alas, who are not so young anymore; they've grown into middle age with me) whom I guided in a very personal way, and thousands whom I had lectured and dialogued with for over thirty years of teaching, many of whom I still hear from who want something else (a letter of recommendation, perhaps) or to just reach out and thank me for my guidance and for being a role model.

You don't make tons of money as a university professor and there's not a lot of prestige in the position anymore, unless you are teaching at an Ivy League school. What you get in academia is a little bit of freedom and flexibility—and the satisfaction of knowing that you have been able to make an impact on a person in transition, like Kathy, trying to change her life and find her voice, who first came to study with me only half a dozen years ago. This is your pay-off as a teacher, all the reward and satisfaction you get—and you don't want it to slip away. You'll not get it back—nor receive it in any other related occupation. The fact that Sam was weakening, I felt then, was a direct reflection on me—and my ability to carve out a man from a boy.

Suddenly, when Sam turned back to resume his cautious descent, he lost his balance, fell and rolled over. I stopped. "Get up," I said, quietly, calmly. "Stand up. Keep going. You're ok."

"I'll stand up when I'm ready, Dad," Sam snapped back.

I took a deep breath and we slogged on in cautious silence to the bottom.

LATER, I ASKED SAM: "Why did you get mad at me on Exit Glacier?"

"You were being kind of aggressive. I have the right to complain. I should be able to say what I want."

"I thought you were getting tired and overwrought. You were reaching your limits."

"Maybe I was. But I'm allowed to express myself, aren't I."

"Yes, and I was wrong for not letting you talk. I'm sorry. I think I lost it a little myself. I was getting tired, too."

"That's ok," said Sam.

"You have to remember that the human being—body and mind—has buckets of reserve buried deep inside and that the feeling of weakness or loss of control should be a red flag to dig in your heels, try harder, and unearth some of that physical and mental reserve. Remember that your mind and body sends you messages," I persisted. "You learn to sense when you are about to reach a point of exhaustion and frustration and prepare yourself for it. This is what I am always trying to teach you. Do you understand all of this? What I am saying?"

"You never give up, do you dad?" Sam said. He was not smiling. "You just keep pushing."

"Yes," I said. "I want you to know who you are—Sam Gutkind—and that you are great. Nobody is better than you. You can be anyone or anything you want to be. You need to know that you can achieve any-thing—I mean *anything*—you want to achieve, as long as you keep trying to do your best."

"Thanks, Dad. I've heard this before. But now," he added, "enough is enough."

Sam was right. And I realized two good things: first, that Sam was winning the inevitable competition of life with his father; he was exerting his will over me, asserting himself, which meant that I was losing a meas-ure of my power and influence over him. And that was one good thing.

But then the other good thing: the fact that Sam was gaining strength, no longer fearing me, no longer subservient to me, meant that I too was winning. I had been successful. I had given Sam or guided Sam toward his own sense of confidence and self-awareness. Not that my job was over as a father—a father's job is never over—and I was too energetic and committed to call it quits. Fatherhood is an ongoing and forever commitment of loyalty and love, no matter how old you are when your phase of fatherhood, new dad or old new dad, begins.

◙ ◙ ◙

And then there was my haunting encounter with the hiker at the edge of the ice field at the glacier's summit. It was after we had eaten our lunch. I was lying on the ground, my eyes closed, soaking up the sun and enjoying the triumphant feeling of satisfaction and accomplishment we shared, when I heard a gravely, elated voice: "What's an old man like you doing all the way up here?"

I opened my eyes. He was a man with gray hair and a gray beard similar to mine, a face creased with wrinkles and a tanned, generous nose, and he was grinning. I stared at him, imagining that my face showed the shock and bewilderment that I was feeling right then.

"We're the two oldest people on top of this glacier by twenty-five years," he said. I looked at him, without speaking, surprised, unwilling and perhaps unable to respond. "You don't belong up here," he continued. "Neither do I, you know what I mean?"

"No," I said. "What do you mean?"

"We're too damn old," he said. "We are not supposed to be able to do what we just did—climb this goddamned mountain!"

He was joking, I knew. He meant no harm. But I did not want Sam or Kathy to think of me as old. I wasn't old at this moment. I felt like a teenager on top of this mountain—or I had felt that way until this old man invaded my space and my elated mood—and spoiled my fantasy.

I looked at this interloper, this grizzled, wrinkled, old codger. I took a deep breath and smiled politely and nodded. Then I closed my eyes and turned away, unable to face the fact that he was, in many ways, a mirror of me.

"You know," he said, calling at me, as I walked away, "I'm about your age and I fought my way up here just like you. I know what it's like—I know how you feel. So I can talk to you that way, can't I?"

"No," I said, turning around once more to face him, "you can't."

The Gödel Connection

PHYSICS, USING SCIENCE to describe the origins and the operation of our universe, has always been a subject of perennial fascination to Sam. Right before he turned fifteen, a year and a half after we returned from Alaska, he began reading in earnest a variety of popular science books, with titles like *A Brief History of Time*, by Stephen Hawking, or *The Elegant Universe*, by Brian Greene. With his interests in mind, a few months earlier I had purchased the fairly recent *A Shortcut Through Time: The Path to the Quantum Computer*, by George Johnson, about an important new subfield in physics known as quantum computing. I began to read it aloud to him during our breakfasts and after-school Starbucks snacks. I understood very little of what Johnson was talking about—reading aloud limits comprehension, and the subject generally eluded me—but Sam was fascinated.

Of the books he was reading his favorite was probably the Pulitzer Prize–winning *Gödel, Escher, Bach: An Eternal Golden Braid*, by Douglas Hofstadter, who described his book as "a metaphorical fugue on minds and machines in the spirit of Lewis Carroll." *GEB*, as it is called, connects the work and ideas of logician Kurt Gödel, artist M. C. Escher, and composer Johann Sebastian Bach and details concepts fundamental to mathematics, symmetry, and intelligence. Its theme centers on how we humans process information and form original thoughts—and it asks the fundamental question of whether consciousness is something unique to humans alone, or whether it may someday emerge in machines.

Kurt Gödel, an Austrian mathematician who lived during the early twentieth century, especially fascinated Sam. He was best known for his incompleteness theorems, which he published when he was twenty-five years old, which demonstrate that no matter how far our mathematical knowledge progresses, there will always be mathematical problems that nobody knows how to solve. Gödel's theorems provoked decades of debate, becoming the basis for many new fields of research, and are now considered among the most important mathematical results ever conceived.

I had never heard of Kurt Gödel, but in my continuing quest to bond with my son and please him in any way possible, I went out and bought Rebecca Goldstein's biography of Gödel, and read that to Sam aloud, quite quickly. It was a great success. In many ways, Gödel was similar to Sam—somewhat of a distracted outsider with his peers, more interested in ideas and intellectual discourse and books than athletics and parties.

Choosing gifts for his birthday and Christmas had always been a chore when Sam was younger, but, now, starting when he was fifteen, books were all that he ever wanted—primarily in the area of mathematics and philosophy, with the natural sciences as supplementary choices. Sitting at his bedside as I write are the following titles: *The Road to Reality-A Complete Guide to the Laws of the Universe*, by Roger Penrose; *Programming the Universe: A Quantum Computer Scientist Takes on the Cosmos*, by Seth Lloyd; *Gödel's Proof*, by Ernest Nagel and James Newman, with a foreword by Douglas Hofstadter; and *The Universe in a Nutshell*, by Stephen Hawking. At this moment we are reading aloud James Gleick's biography of Isaac Newton. What amazes and impresses me about Sam is that he really believes in books generally—they are evidence of something that is real and solid in this world, a foundation of knowledge without spin or duplicity, such as we see each night as, sporadically, we watch CNN or read from the New York Times.

Two years ago, I contacted Rebecca Goldstein, who teaches in Cambridge, Massachusetts, and is also a novelist and philosopher, and explained Sam's interest in her work and in Gödel, and asked if I could bring him up for an interview that summer. Rebecca, impressed with Sam, recommended that he also visit the philosopher Gregory Chaitin, one of IBM's super thinkers, the author of *Meta Math*, also on Sam's bookshelf, which mixes mathematics with Chaitin's outlook on life and philosophy and includes deep chunks of narrative and opinion about Kurt Gödel and Albert Einstein, Gödel's good friend. Flamboyant and outspoken in real life, Chaitin writes the way he speaks. When he wants to emphasize a word or sentence—or an entire section—he prints it in bold, as if he is declaring himself—loudly and with clarity—in a church or library. *Meta Math* is organized randomly, which reflects his work on randomness in mathematics—also, as it turns out, the way he lives his life.

Sam e-mailed Chaitin and made an appointment, and I drove him up to IBM's Watson Research Center, located near Hawthorne, New York. Perhaps because Sam did not tell him—or perhaps because he didn't read Sam's e-mail carefully enough—Chaitin had no idea that Sam was a high-school student, for he had planned, we discovered, to have Sam join him to drink and party. I had not intended to go to the lunch; I was to drop Sam off and hide away somewhere in town until the interview was over and he called for me. This was to be Sam's gig.

But for once Sam was lucky to have a bothersome, outgoing father, for I drank the wine, ate the exotic dishes ordered up at the Portuguese restaurant Chaitin had picked out, and kept the discussion going when Sam's interview techniques faltered. Sam's interview continued a few hours later, after our lunch, when Chaitin suddenly proposed an afternoon hike up to a ridge overlooking the Hudson River, where, he promised, we'd see the skyline of Manhattan (we didn't; a haze blanketed the distant city). I will never forget watching Sam, thin and lanky, as he followed the great stout philosopher in his Australian bush cowboy hat, trudging up and down the mountain and holding his tape recorder high over head, capturing Chaitin's every word as he pontificated randomly, as in *Meta Math,* about Gödel, Von Neumann, Descartes, Charles Johnson—and the dying embers of the age of philosopher-scientists like himself.

During our talk at the Portuguese restaurant and our hike, Chaitin suggested that Sam also reach out to another mathematician, somewhat of a maverick—Stephen Wolfram. Interestingly, Rebecca Goldstein had also suggested Wolfram as a person Sam should interview. Chaitin reiterated the idea of Sam meeting Wolfram at the end of the hike, although he said he wondered whether Wolfram, who had become a very busy and important man, would make the time to see a kid like Sam. Chaitin underestimated my son.

Eventually, Chaitin led us back to his home, nestled on a quiet street at the edge of town, to view his collection of artwork—paintings, sculptures, and drawings—mostly nudes. It was good for Sam to see that even the most distinguished philosophers in the world could, on occasion, ponder the complexities and beauty of the female form. Later that summer we were to visit Princeton University, where Sam devoted a day to exploring the Gödel archives. We visited Gödel's grave, which, coincidently, was near Von Neumann's burial spot. We joined dozens of other mysterious Gödel devotees, placing a tiny pebble on Gödel's headstone.

THE YEAR SAM discovered *Gödel, Escher, Bach* and *A Shortcut Through Time*, Sam and I were also training for the Marine Corps Marathon. We had been talking about doing a marathon over the past year as if it were some distant dream, but suddenly, out of the blue, one day after running twelve miles and feeling pretty energetic at the end, Sam realized that he could probably, with a bit of pushing and pain, run twelve or fourteen more miles. And we did, in November 2005, crossing the finish line with an average of eleven minutes per mile—not too shabby for one of the hundred youngest kids running that day in a field of twenty-two thousand. Not bad for an old man, like me, either.

It is interesting to me—and very satisfying—that Sam is the one person in the world who never thinks of me, as far as I can discern, as old. Personally, I doubted whether I could finish the Marine Corps Marathon—but finishing for either of us was never in doubt in Sam's mind. The question to answer was always, for Sam, how fast we could run the marathon and what we would have to eat while carbo-loading. But never a doubt or question that it could be done; this was something we would do together—of course.

I remember that when we crossed the finish line that day, I began to cry—to weep, deeply—with relief and pride, for us both. He looked at me—it was a double-take—first with surprise, and then, quickly, with kindness and understanding. I will never forget the empathy in his eyes at that moment, as we stood at the finish line, listening to the din of the cheering crowd, giving thanks for the strength of our own bodies and the power of our bonding spirit. We ran the Marine Corps Marathon together, side-by-side, and we have run two marathons since, the Pittsburgh Marathon and Run Vermont in Burlington. But in both cases, Sam was way out ahead of me. His Pittsburgh time was an hour faster than mine.

WE ACTUALLY TRAINED for the Marine Corps Marathon in the summer in Madrid, in 90-plus degree heat, where I was teaching for a month. We returned to Madrid for another month in 2006, where we traveled extensively throughout the country, including a visit to Pamplona—where we did not run with the bulls. This may have been a mistake; we were, after all, in the heart of Hemingway country—a place and a time where machismo and male bonding was at the height of tradition and chic. I thought about the wisdom of running with the bulls for a long time, wrestled with the pros and cons of Sam and his Dad being able to boast about this achievement for the rest of our lives, with Sam telling his kids, "I ran with the bulls like Hemingway did in Pamplona—me and my dad!" Sam was ambivalent; if I did it, he would do it. And if not, well, that was okay with him, as well.

The night before the running, I found myself in the Café Iruña in the Plaza de Castillo, Hemingway's hangout in Pamplona, watching a young American student, whose name was Pete. It was five o'clock in the morning, three hours before the running of the bulls. Sam was in bed, but I was roaming the square, looking for I don't know what. Pete was dancing with a manic intensity, waving his scarlet scarf, twirling it and pretending to swallow it and pulling it out of his mouth like a carnival sword-swallower and shaking his fat body. He dropped down on his stomach and slid, his white pants soaking in the layer of slime of wine and beer and cigarette butts, along the floor. Outside, an American girl named Jennifer, only a few years older than my Sam, was sitting in the grass, crying. Chick, her companion, was lying in a lump in his sleeping bag shaking from whatever chemical he had taken. "Where are their parents?" I remember thinking to myself, as I headed back to my hotel. "Why aren't they at home? This is not right, I think."

I know what I did when I was their ages, where I went and how I behaved, all my wild motorcycle days, and in the long run it didn't hurt me, I guess, but I didn't want Sam to take the chances that I took or to be a part of these revelers. I didn't want Sam to drink and get drunk, to experiment with drugs, to party like Pete in the Iruna or cry on the grass in the middle of the Plaza de Castillo.

Such mixed feelings. Experience versus restraint. Where is the line? I asked myself. By the time I returned to the hotel to wake Sam, the line, to me, was clear. (We wanted an early start if we were to run with the bulls or get a good seat on the fence and watch them thunder by.) The experience of trying to run a marathon—or of driving across the tundra—in a Tundra—was significantly different, goal-oriented, potentially productive. Driving the AlCan, we would get to Alaska, we would see sights, climb mountains, meet interesting people. There was a substantial reward to it, as there was the physical and emotional satisfaction of running 26.2 miles without stopping.

I wasn't certain I could say that about running with the bulls in Pamplona. I asked myself, as I made my way back to the hotel, dodging the drunken revelers, how would I—or could I?—justify my actions and decisions if either I or Sam were seriously injured—or worse—while dashing through the narrow alleyways of Pamplona? How could I answer the people who knew and loved us, or my own conscience, when the question was posed: What were you thinking? Why did you do it?

Because it was there? Because Hemingway did it—and romanticized it for the world? That was not a good enough justification. I want my son to be daring and courageous, and I want my son to know not only how to take chances in life—but when.

I THOUGHT OF THAT early morning in Pamplona and all of the key and significant decisions that I have made for and with my son and the rich and sometimes dicey experiences we shared, as I stared across the room in the dark in Lhasa, Tibet, that night in mid-March 2008.

The gunshots had subsided by then, the soldiers no longer visible, the din and clamor of the neighborhood settling into a temporary lull brought on by the dawn.

This trip to Tibet was an experience we had looked forward to for a long time—"to go somewhere near the end of the world, where few Westerners ever venture"—that was our goal. We had reached the destination, but not achieved the goal, in a sense. We were in Tibet; we had had a taste of it and we wanted much more. We were supposed to visit, among other destinations, the Mt. Everest Base Camp—a specific choice and request from Sam.

But I knew, as I sat there by the window watching my son sleep, that it was a choice I could not honor—as much as I wanted to fulfill the acronym AFS (Anything for Sam) whenever possible. Gunshots and soldiers equipped with weapons and riot gear, in a country where no one speaks your language and laowai are considered interlopers, as they were by the Chinese military, who were trying to keep the insurrection a secret to the outside world, is not a place to take chances.

A few decades ago, I might have looked at things differently; I wanted all of the experiences I could get, and I felt, quite literally, unflappable and untouchable. Nothing could happen to me; bad stuff happens to other people. And if something did happen, I would be the only person to suffer the loss. So who, really, would care?

Now, older and wiser and not so foolhardy or adventurous, the word "loss" took on another meaning. The "loss" I could suffer could be my son, and my son could suffer the "loss" of me. My son would survive without me in the long run—I have given him almost everything I have to give. But I have no right to make decisions that would endanger him. Clint Eastwood could make his day and Burt Reynolds could indeed do something because it is there to do, but not Lee Gutkind, even though, perhaps, it makes me seem old and a little frightened and over the hill and not as manly or free-spirited as I once thought myself to be. Besides, we are talking movies—not real life.

As it turned out, I was right to have been a little frightened. Getting through the angry crowds on the street the following morning on Beijing Middle Road, slipping past the soldiers in their riot gear surrounding the neighborhood of the hated Han, required a cadre of escorts, provided by the hotel and the Tibetan Travel Bureau. We were then convoyed to the airport, along with a dozen other Western tourists and, elbowing our way through the manic, pressured crowds, we were put on the first available flight out of the country.

We left Tibet with relief—but also a feeling of loss that we were unable to fulfill the promise of our most recent and exotic adventure. The decision to leave—against the advice of our guide, who had advised us to stay another twenty-four hours and then reevaluate our plans—turned out to be wise. The day after we left, angry crowds stormed through the soldiers blockade and trashed our neighborhood.

Leaving Lhasa, we ended up in Beijing, where we toured the important sights—the Great Wall, the Forbidden City, Tiananmen Square—for a few days before returning home. "It was fortunate that we decided to leave Lhasa when we did," I told Sam, later, when we finally headed back to the United States. "We were in the midst of a revolution."

"It was a religious experience," said Sam. "Most revolutions are religious experiences," he added.

A few months later, while watching CNN's ongoing coverage of the turmoil in Tibet, we saw to our surprise our former guide, Tenzin, being interviewed. He was identified by his first and last name, Tenzin Choeying, which we had not known, and referred to as one of the leaders of the uprising.

That was pretty exciting—and surprising.

That same year we went to the Czech Republic, Poland, Germany, and Israel, which was when we visited Auschwitz, Theiresentadt, Berlin, Prague, and Israeli-occupied Hebron in the troubled and volatile West Bank. This year, 2009, it is Africa, biking across part of Tanzania and climbing Mt. Kilimanjaro—Sam and ancient me, continuing to follow the truckin' tradition. How much longer will we truck together? I guess this is up to Sam, who may well choose other traveling companions and different destinations as he grows older. I am hoping to hang in and be a part of his life for as long as possible, but I know that Sam has his future, wherever that takes him—college and beyond now. And I have my memories.

Afterword

By Sam Gutkind

ONE FALL DAY in 2006, as I was browsing the science bookshelves at a local Barnes and Noble, which I tended to do after coming out of the nearby movie theater that I frequently visited, I came across an encyclopedic, twelve-hundred-page tome nestled among the collage of popular science books. I looked in the flaps:

> This long-awaited work from one of the world's most respected scientists presents a series of dramatic discoveries never before made public. . . . [The author] uses his approach to tackle a remarkable array of fundamental problems in science, from the origins of apparent randomness in physical systems, to the development of complexity in biology, the ultimate scope and limitations of mathematics, the possibility of a truly fundamental theory of physics, the interplay between free will and determinism, and the character of intelligence in the universe.

This was Stephen Wolfram's *A New Kind of Science*, the subject of a great deal of praise and controversy in the computer science field, as I would soon discover. I had only heard of Wolfram's book in passing, in a bibliographic reference at the end of another popular science book I had read a few months earlier. The book's description intrigued me, however—many of the subjects it mentions had already been topics of interest to me—and so I decided to look it up on Wikipedia.

Wolfram, an Oxford scholar who published his first paper on particle physics at fifteen, had devoted more than ten years to this project. His inspiration, he said, had come when a computer program he had written began to display random, seemingly garbled output. When he checked it, however, all the code he had written had been correct. The program itself had generated this bizarre output all on its own. Wolfram began a study of how processes across all fields of science—computer programs, fluid waves, plant cells, and human thoughts—could produce complexity out of nothing, developing intricate facets and features for no obvious mathematical reason. The result of this monumental study was *A New Kind of Science*.

It was not for another year and a half—the end of my junior year—that I actually finished the book. This has actually been a common practice for me; my bedside table is often piled with six or seven books that I have started then abandoned in favor of another book, intending to resume it later. Even Douglas Hofstadter's *Gödel, Escher, Bach*, one of the main books that launched my interest in mathematical logic, had taken me almost two years to finish. The real problem is that I suffer from an intense myopia of interest. At any given time, I am contemplating only one or two or three questions, usually philosophical dilemmas having to do with free will, or metaphysical concerns about how the laws of physics came into being; and then I become obsessed with these problems, unable to muster the focus to do so much as read a paragraph on any other subject. I come into a book wanting new insight on one particular question I am pondering, and I lack the patience to follow the author if he drifts off into discussing something else.

In many ways I have the same problem with school. Even in high school, about three quarters of my classes are required; I take them because I have to. I am often astounded by the contrast between the original and creative thinking I feel myself doing, the deep questions I am able to ask, when I am reading about something to indulge my fascination; and the tedious monotony of the busywork I am assigned. I complete these assignments for one reason: the grades I earn on them are essentially the only way for me to prove to our educational system that I am intelligent and academically competent enough to merit acceptance to a good college.

The most striking example of this irony is perhaps my gym class, which I have been forced to take for the past two years in order to earn my diploma. Each day, the teacher takes attendance and awards full credit to students as long as they change into their gym clothes and participate in class activities—usually only a short warm-up consisting of thirty push-ups and sit-ups. After that, students are allowed to do whatever they want—to play hockey, basketball, or some invented sport involving hurtling the orange field-hockey balls at one another—or, my personal choice, to walk around idly in circles and try to think. The only rule: students are forbidden to sit down, read, or work on their schoolwork, at any time.

Perhaps my teachers believe that they are doing me a favor when they assign me thirty redundant problems each night and expect me to complete them for the next day. My senior-year physics teacher was often frustrated by the fact that her students preferred exchanging anecdotes about our weekends to doing homework problems and watching her derivations on the board. One morning, sensing our frustration with her nightly homework assignments, she recounted to us one of her experiences at the University of Chicago. In preparation for one of her exams, she had completed all of the two hundred practice problems her teacher had given her. She wound up second in her class.

All I can say is that, while this philosophy works for some people, it is unbelievably presumptuous for educators to assign their students such large workloads before making sure it will work for them as well. In many cases, it does nothing except squander students' motivation and show them that academia is a waste of time. High-school science and math teachers almost invariably assault their students with a barrage of objective questions that can be answered by taking some procedure learned in class and applying it repeatedly, over and over, to more and more situations posed in the problems. This kind of repetitious style of practice might be well suited for training assembly-line workers—but it is never the way real academic research is done. Researchers are motivated by the potential to be creative, to make discoveries that have never been made before, and to be recognized for it. I always wanted the opportunity to do something like this in high school. I wanted to read as many books as I could about mathematical logic, to seek out unanswered questions, to write computer programs that would uncover the answers, and to share my questions, results, and discoveries with the research community online. But I was barred the opportunity to do this because my teachers determined that my time would be better spent relearning material I had studied months ago so that I could pass the Advanced Placement exam.

It was in the midst of this turmoil that I began to consider the *New Kind of Science* Summer School, a three-week workshop hosted by Stephen Wolfram and some of his top researchers, held at the beginning of every summer. I had already learned of the workshop about a year before—only a few months after that initial day in the bookstore when I first discovered *A New Kind of Science* (I had purchased it the next day). But I had never seriously considered applying—at the time, I had only read a few chapters and wasn't sure about my direction towards math and logic. Now, by the middle of my junior year, having already taken an introductory course on mathematical reasoning at Carnegie Mellon University, and having had another year to foment my contempt for the educational system, I began to realize that I knew enough to conduct my own research project, which I would have to present at the end of the workshop. The Summer School's website stated that most of their participants were advanced undergraduates, but that they would accept applications from anyone, and had in fact had some "exceptional high-school age students" in the past. I decided to give it a try. I filled out an application, including a short essay in which I focused on how I wanted to present Wolfram's ideas to a wider audience of students in my high school, especially prospective researchers and engineers.

As part of the application process, the Summer School had a policy of conducting an on-the-phone interview with every applicant they were seriously considering. For me, this interview took place at the beginning of March, while I was in China with my dad. I would be speaking with Todd Rowland, the academic director of the Summer School. He had been an important research assistant to Stephen Wolfram, instrumental in clearing up the mathematical issues in key parts of *A New Kind of Science*. I received a call from him one Wednesday morning, in our Chengdu apartment. He said I had written an interesting application and asked me a few more practical details about myself: what were my career interests, what kind of project was I interested in pursuing, what were my favorite chapters in *A New Kind of Science*—the things I hadn't talked about in my application. The entire interview took barely fifteen minutes. I received my final letter of acceptance the next day, when I checked my e-mail after arriving at the hotel in Tibet.

The Summer School, which took place at the University of Vermont in Burlington, was comprised in large part of discussions, lectures, and interactive computer demonstrations, in which Wolfram and several other instructors would use a giant projected screen to show off programs they had written that would illustrate or resolve some mathematical issue. These affairs would often run from nine o'clock in the morning to ten at night, excluding generous breaks for lunch and dinner, as well as some intermittent snack breaks.

As the highlight of the Summer School, however, each student was expected to complete an original research project on some issue having to do with computer programs and the mathematics surrounding them, which they would then present to the other participants. Most of these projects consisted of writing some computer program in *Mathematica*, a programming language developed by Wolfram's company, in order to find the answer to some unresolved mathematical question. We had already received training materials to teach us to program in *Mathematica*, as well as a free copy of the software to install on our computers. The next step was to choose a specific topic to research. To accomplish this, each student was scheduled for a half-hour private session with Stephen Wolfram.

My first interaction with Wolfram actually came on the very first day, during which I and four other students were scheduled to share a two-hour lunch with him. Walking to the restaurant, Wolfram and I introduced ourselves to one another. After I told him I was in high school, he asked me what other high-school students were like. I didn't know what to say, except to say that they were not like me: very few people in my class actually know what it is mathematicians do, let alone share my passion that their field is the irreducible essence of all knowledge. At lunch, Wolfram began by asking us what kinds of projects we planned to do. Two of the students were linguistics majors from New York University, and so the conversation quickly evolved into a discussion of that field, with Wolfram pondering which human languages have a word for the logical concept of 'exclusive or,' and commenting on the way new English words are formed from the names of commercial products. Wolfram speaks in the way much of *A New Kind of Science* is written, supplying the conversation with an endless stream of offhand anecdotes and questions about almost any subject that arises.

That night, I was scheduled for my private meeting with Wolfram in which we would lay out the plan for my project. At nine-thirty, I left the lecture hall and walked upstairs into a quiet office, seating myself at a table across from Wolfram, with Hector Zenil, the instructor who would be supervising my project, sitting to my left. Wolfram asked me what I wanted to do my research on.

Ever since the middle of my freshman year in high school, when I learned about Gödel's incompleteness theorems, mathematics has more or less been the only thing I have been passionate about. Since I was nine years old, I have been struggling with the question of what it really means for human beings to possess consciousness, and whether or not there is such a thing as free will. I have always been curious about what it means for us to live in a universe governed by the laws of physics. Deep down, so far as scientists can tell, everything that happens in the universe, everything we do, is a consequence of tiny subatomic particles bouncing off one another, colliding, turning into other particles, and doing all this according to a set of rules, like the rules in a board game. Hofstadter, in *Gödel, Escher, Bach*, ingeniously casts the issue of consciousness in a new light by looking at it in terms of Gödel's incompleteness theorems. In the course of a year or two, I came to the realization that all of these unanswerable questions that have haunted me for so many years might really be answered by looking at them in terms of mathematics. It has been for this reason that I have sought out book after book on math and physics, why I was so enthralled when I saw *A New Kind of Science* that day in the bookstore, and why I pursued the Summer School, my desire to know the truth about these fundamental questions unrelenting and thoroughly unsatisfied.

I should have known that finding answers to these questions was too much to ask of one research project in a three-week summer program. When I told Wolfram, in a few words, the general idea of what I had on my mind, he came up with a series of computer experiments I could carry out, drawing diagrams on sheets of paper for added clarification. It would be an extension of the work he had done in one section of his book. It was clear enough what I would have to do: I would need to write a computer program that would carry out the kinds of experiments and calculations that Wolfram had suggested.

Wolfram's proposal was straightforward—but too straightforward. Besides chugging away at my computer for a few afternoons at the local coffee shop, there wasn't too much more I would have to do. Wolfram's proposal asked a specific mathematical question, and once I had written the computer program that would give me the answer, though it may satisfy Wolfram, I would hardly be any closer to a resolution of those lofty philosophical dilemmas than when I had begun. It would not satisfy me. I wanted to struggle—to formulate an ambitious project and then to struggle for hours on end, staring at a blank sheet of paper, hands wrapped around my head; to assault my problem with idea after idea after idea, pouring out an endless stream of ingenious workarounds that would bring me closer to seeing into the mathematical heart of the issue, only to watch them fall apart, and then to try again. Albert Einstein spent over six years dedicated to working out the general theory of relativity, all because he couldn't quite get the math to work out. I had decided I was ready for the same thing myself.

Unfortunately, I have come to realize, that is seldom the way science is done nowadays. After the meeting with Wolfram, in which I had voiced none of my inner discontent, I spoke to Todd Rowland and asked if I could broaden the scope of my project. He insisted that I would have to start simple. While I might like to ask a much less specific, more fundamental question, he said, it would make my project too complicated to hope to achieve in three weeks. We went out for coffee and spent about an hour talking. He didn't change my opinion about anything, except that by the end, I was willing to accept the fact that, since I had no plan whatsoever for carrying out the kind of project I was talking about, I would have to set my philosophical ambitions to the side for another three weeks and stick with what I knew how to do.

I did in fact spend a few hours in the coffee shop staring at a blank sheet of paper with my hands wrapped around my head, anyway. Developing a computer program that did exactly what I wanted was a challenge, and I had the opportunity to come up with my own unique way of solving it. On the final day of the Summer School, the participants filled the room with posters to present the work they did. Todd suggested that, if I just expanded my project a bit, I might be able to publish my results in an academic journal. I didn't achieve in three weeks the philosophical breakthroughs that I will probably spend the rest of my life searching for, but this is not to be expected when one is conducting real science.

Uhuru

Africa—July 2009

THE REGULAR PROGRAM we had signed up for calls for a four-night, five-day climb of Kilimanjaro up the "Marungu"—or "Coca Cola"—route. Our group had chosen to pay an extra $250 for the "Machame" ("whiskey") route. Although more difficult, it allows climbers another day to adjust to the altitude and to make their way more slowly to the top. There were four guides to lead us, a chief cook and his assistant, and more than a dozen porters to carry our gear and set up and take down our camp. We ate tasty, hot meals three times a day—plus tea with freshly popped popcorn or cookies waiting at camp in the afternoon.

As he had vowed earlier, Sam was not giving in to his injuries and not giving up on the mountain. He was persevering. Exactly a week after the crash, after four days of hiking, we crawled out of our tents at Barafu camp, the highest camp on the Machame route. It was midnight, and we were wearing nearly every piece of clothing we had brought with us. We gulped down mugs of hot tea and began the final seven-kilometer, six-hour ascent to the top: Uhuru Point.

The challenge of Kilimanjaro is not technical; it is a test of fortitude and commitment that requires walking (and sometimes crawling) over roots, rocks, gravel—sharply upward and painfully downward and then up again. The high altitude can be crippling. Some of us suffered from nausea and headaches, despite the Diamox—medication to stabilize the effects of the height. "Polepole" (slowly) were the watchwords for the climb. Those who go up the mountain too fast are usually the ones who fail to reach the top.

I was very cold when we started up the mountain from Barafu camp. At first my hands and toes ached and then, after a few hours walking into the biting wind, I couldn't feel my hands or feet at all. The curtain of darkness beyond my headlamp's beam made me feel eerie and disengaged.

More than thirty thousand people come from all over the world every year to climb Kilimanjaro. That night there were perhaps four hundred people trying to reach the summit—crowding, fighting to stay together, and conversing in a dozen different languages. I passed many struggling climbers, exhausted and detached. I saw an older woman stumble to the ground and claw frantically like an animal to get to her feet—unsuccessfully. A younger woman was sobbing "I can't" to her friend, who was hugging her. A man was doubled over; he couldn't stop coughing.

All the way up the mountain—five nights and six days—and especially on that early morning struggle the last day, I thought of Exit Glacier. Not that Exit Glacier was more difficult than Kilimanjaro—not at all; there was no comparison. But Exit Glacier was Sam's first long trek—and his first real assertion of himself, measuring up against me. Since Exit Glacier we have had many mountains to climb—treks that were tests—physically and intellectually.

In addition to the Colorado Trail, the Great Wall in China, Havasupai Canyon in the Grand Canyon, there was the Marine Corps Marathon when was Sam was 14, moving to another town and adjusting to another school (we had temporarily relocated to Arizona), confrontations with bullies in his last year of middle school—and the constant discipline of reading and studying, in isolation, in order to be accepted by those he aspired to emulate, like Chaitin and Wolfram and Rebecca Goldstein. These challenges, problems to solve, goals to achieve, were all mountains to conquer or, perhaps, to make peace with—just like biking across Tanzania and triumphing over Kilimanjaro. In some respects, Africa was a culmination—a transition into adulthood.

But this is the rhythm and reality of life I have always been trying to talk to Sam about: Aspire to greatness, acknowledge and respect life's difficulties—never give up or give in easily—not until you recognize that giving up can lead to other options and opportunities. It is a question of confidence, of knowing who you are and having faith in your own abilities. Hakuna matata, the Africans would say, which, in some respects, was like truckin'—going with the flow, adjusting to events, trusting your ideas and feelings.

For a while that dark frozen morning, I followed Sam—even in the blackness I could recognize him because he was limping. He had been

limping from the moment we left the hospital a week ago—our porters were convinced that he would never make it past the first day. But he was hanging in—which is exactly what I was trying desperately to do as I crept upward through the night. I was bone tired and gasping for air, each breath exploding with pain in my chest. I remember thinking, "I will not give up. I will do this, placing one foot ahead of the other until I collapse or die." I made it alive—but barely—in a little over six hours, about an hour after a brilliant sunrise.

I caught up with my limping son and we trudged together forty minutes to the famous sign at the summit that all climbers seek to document their victory over the mountain at Uhuru. Our guide, Rumi, found us and took our picture, and Sam and I tried to cheer and celebrate. But we were both too cold and tired at that moment to feel the elation we had expected and desired.

And besides, there was no time to celebrate or rest and recuperate. It was a long way back down—longer even than going up, for after we returned to Barafu camp and ate some lunch, we would hike an additional seven miles down to the next camp where we would spend that night.

But at that point we were too numb to think seriously about that upcoming challenge. We knew we would do it somehow. Limping or gasping, or even crawling, we'd get there. Rumi expressed our sentiments with a casual shrug as we started down the mountain. "Hakuna matata," he said.

Truckin'

A Final Word

SO MUCH ABOUT Sam's growth and maturity has been a delightful mystery to me, his obsession with computers first of all, when he was only four years old, transitioning into his obsession with gaming, evolving into his intense devotion to mathematics and physics—and the deep questions he is asking and attempting with enthusiasm and impatience to answer.

The transition happened right in front of my eyes, at home, where he hid away in his room for long hours, reading and then carefully annotating ideas and observations from the books he was reading. While truckin', it took me a long time to realize what was happening when Sam was so removed, staring glassy-eyed straight ahead through the windshield for hours on end as we were riding the road and listening to rock and roll. Sam wasn't spacing out; rather, he was digging in, so to speak—analyzing, contemplating, speculating, and hypothesizing. His interest in long-distance running makes perfect sense in this context, for it allows him to continue to meditate and establish a satisfying and productive mind-body connection.

Sam changed right in front of my eyes as we lived and trucked together over the past decade. I knew it was happening—I was helping it to happen, knowingly—but it only really became clear when certain events occurred, like when he caught up to me during my crazed Exit Glacier dash, or those times when he confronted me and refused to allow me to force my will upon him, whether I was right or wrong—

and when he writes such meaningful and heartfelt reflections, as in the afterword, here. Sam is no longer a child, no longer my boy. He's his own man. What happened in Africa made this reality indisputably evident.

And yet—

There was this night truckin' in Nebraska I will never forget, rocketing through the pitch blackness, listening to Mick Jagger croon and belt the oldies but goodies like "You Can't Always Get What You Want" and "High Wire" and "Like a Rolling Stone."

In the truck, Sam was by my side. We were holding hands, and he was smiling that kindly solicitous, toothless smile that he always flashes to assure me that he/everything was all right and we were doing good truckin' through the wee hours of the night.

We didn't know where we were going at that moment or when we might try to stop. We had our truck, our Rolling Stones, and our anonymity—we had the vast and endless open road, and we had each other. As far as I was concerned, I didn't ever want to stop, didn't ever need to stop. My little Sam was with me. I loved him more than anything or anybody I had ever conceived of loving. Sam was my dream-come-true of a lifetime. I didn't need or want anything or anybody else, then or forever more.

Sam, my son and my beloved, was all there was or ever would be. The darkness of the night and the vast emptiness of the country and the intimacy of the cab was everything I had ever wanted. I was on edge because of the driving, energized just enough to keep me alert and feeling adventurous. Sam was close. His velvety fingertips were brushing against mine. I was totally, unbelievably, irrevocably filled with joy for and appreciation of the fruits of fatherhood. Nothing could have been better, more satisfying, more exhilarating, more pristine.

I remember that moment, the most meaningful moment of my life, in many respects, for I realized then what exactly truckin' with Sam symbolized for me: his love. Not my love and devotion for him, which is the selfish, egoistic anchor of our experiences, but his love for me. Through all of this time, raising Sam, mentoring Sam, counseling Sam, confronting Sam, and capitulating to Sam, my son has put himself in my hands, honoring me and relying on me. His trust and loyalty are both true testaments of his faith in and love for me, his father.

Does God exist?

I only know that I am blessed.

Acknowledgments

OUR BONDING ADVENTURES—and this book—have been shaped and fortified by the genius and spirit of Bob Dylan, Mick Jagger, The Grateful Dead, The Doors, The Who, The Band, Dire Straits, and many others, as well as Jack Kerouac, Peter Fonda, Ernest Hemingway, Lauren Slater, Kurt Godel, the mathematician Stephen Wolfram, and Charlie the short-order cook.

Drafts of this book have been reviewed and shaped by two wonderful writers: Meredith Hall and Pagan Kennedy. Parts of this book were written while I served as Virginia G. Piper Distinguished Writer in Residence at Arizona State University. I wish to thank the Virginia G. Piper Center for Creative Writing for its support.

We also want to acknowledge our editor, James Peltz, for his patience and trust; senior production editor Kelli Williams-LeRoux, for her cooperation; and especially our agent, Andrew Blauner, whose faith in our work never wavered.